The seven birthstones

A mother's heartache and loss

Nicole Narracott

First published in 2020.

Cover design by Sam Kness

www.mumstheword.blog

ISBN: 978-1-8382164-0-5

To Paulo who carefully and lovingly picked up the pieces
of my heart every time it shattered.

Also to Tilly and Chloe for making my heart smile
when nothing else could.

Contents

Table of Contents

Why read my story?

This book started as a diary, which I intended to give to my child, when I was planning single motherhood, to explain my choice and journey to have them. The diary changed as hurdles changed to loss and longing changed to grief. I have added excerpts of this diary directly into the book, to show my thoughts and feelings at the time.

This has been a very long journey. The first entry in the diary was dated 24th March 2007, as I make my final edits, it is June 2020, although the book ends at the start of 2019. My quest for motherhood dates from even further back, when I didn't realise how much can get in the way of the normal, everyday event of becoming a mum. I also never realised I'd face travelling so much of this journey alone.

In this book I use the word infertility as unable to get pregnant as well as unable to carry a child to term.

There are many reasons for infertility. The NHS define this as when a couple are unable to conceive. However, there are a growing amount of groups who relate to the word infertility. There is secondary infertility where you are unable to conceive after having no issues the first time; there is social infertility, where your biology may work fine but you are single therefore unable to conceive. Its use and our understanding of related issues is growing and therefore I suspect it will keep changing as a definition of a condition.

Infertility is regarded as a disease because it needs medication to treat it. It is deemed no less than a disability in that it is a chronic condition which meets the biopsychological social role and legal criteria for disability. In 2016 the WHO claimed that singledom was a disability, in order to allow more single people across the world to access fertility treatment.

I use the word in the way I can relate to it. Others may perceive its definition differently. Either way, infertility is crushingly unfair and still very misunderstood. To want what so many take for granted. To want what should just happen, what biology dictates, what no creature on earth seems to struggle with. What every couple on the TV programme, Grand Designs, seem to end the show with, along with a massive new house. A baby.

Infertility changes you. It impacts your mental health. There are unavoidable triggers everywhere. You can easily be overcome by your emotions. Not many of the books I have read talk about the dark places you can go to; they touch on it and then get to the happy ending. Infertility has changed me and changed how I feel about myself. I always felt I was a mother, to not be one took away a huge part of who I was. It impacted my identity and my confidence. It impacted connections I had with friends. I lost my place in the world, my footing. Most books are written once a happy ending has been achieved. I struggled to relate to these books, and I craved to find someone who understood.

It has felt like a lonely place to be, with sometimes little empathy or understanding and I am hoping that this look into my inner world, can bring some comfort to people in knowing they are not alone. Hopefully also to help explain this unwanted journey I have found myself on, to those who are lucky enough to never tread its path, and finally, to give a voice to those yet to find their happy ending.

The five-year plan

Unlike many little girls, I never really dreamt about a prince or a wedding, although I did assume it would happen, I also thought I'd probably end up divorced. For a long time, I was a pretty ardent feminist and believed I would be a career woman with no man holding me back. I saw men as a barrier to freedom. Perhaps because of my strained relationship with my dad and the way I perceived my mum's life as a housewife.

However, since before I can remember, probably from the first time I ever held a doll, I knew I was going to be a mum. It just felt natural. Looking back to all the games I played, I always had children. I would walk around the garden with my pram and babies, feeding them, dressing them, playing schools, reading them stories, loving them. I was always drawn to babies, with a natural urge to hold them, care for them and protect them. Whenever there was a baby, I couldn't tear my eyes away, I wanted to be involved. I knew that motherhood was a part of me.

For a while, this was not a priority, I wanted to be young and free and enjoy myself, perhaps travel, have a career. I knew that I wasn't going to have children before having my degree and not going to Uni was never in question, although what to do with my degree once I had it, remained a question, even for many years after I had it. I was always quite sure that, should I happen to get pregnant before then, I would terminate the pregnancy as this was best for everyone concerned. I did not feel responsible enough for a child but also, I did not want to be held back from my freedom.

My parents got together, quite late in life and, in my eyes, just to have children, which in my childish view of their relationship, I always felt was entirely the wrong reason to be with someone. I felt it should all be about the two of you, the romance and the love. My dad, Tony, was a teacher and had been working in Switzerland where he met my mum, Lotte, who was a nurse and passionate about her career. They were married in Switzerland but shortly afterwards moved to England where my father had a new teaching position. My mum hadn't known a word of English when she first came over but learnt it listening to the Cricket on the radio and watching children's television with us. They both agreed that my mum would not go to work.

They were already pretty old, compared to the norm, by the time they had my sister, Julie and two years later, had me. My mum had a miscarriage between us two and told us about it. The doctor had told her "you can try again" and that comforted her. They did and all was fine. With her nursing background, my mum never held back from telling us the truth about what happens in life. She explained that there must have been a reason the baby hadn't survived and I came to the conclusion that a miscarriage was something you just dealt with, because in the grand scheme of things it was probably for the best and should I ever have one, I would be fine and my other children would ensure that.

My mum and dad were very different to other parents. I was teased a lot about my 'Grandma' coming to pick me up from school. Possibly their age was more obvious back then. I was born a couple of months before my mum's 41st birthday and my dad had just turned 46. In the mid-late 1970's I think this was very unusual. Fertility treatment was unheard of, so I suspect other couples who met later on may simply not have been able to get pregnant. People do seem to remain young for longer now and also have children later. There are a lot more options also to support older couples in having a family.

At the time, I could feel the difference in the small details of life, in what we did at the weekends, what we watched on telly, what my parents listened to on the radio. Because of this, I felt like I never quite fitted in. I'd go to birthday parties and other people's homes were so different, in the furniture, the colours, everything. An example would be the fact we never had a sofa, something which seems so normal. We had two wing-back armchairs and one wing-back two-seater. There was no slouching or lying in front of the telly in our house. My mum wasn't keen we watch any television at all and definitely nothing that wasn't on the BBC. My friend's parents, seemed so young and fashionable, dads wearing jeans and tee-shirts, mums with 80's perms. My dad was always dressed smartly. He thought tee-shirts were underwear and would always wear a shirt, even to do the gardening, although he would remove his tie and roll up his sleeves to mow the lawn. He would spend hours polishing all our shoes on a Friday night so they looked smart for the following week. My mum wore her hair in a very traditional bun and always wore skirts or dresses, since my dad disapproved of women in trousers. She was always very elegant, and co-ordinated her jewellery beautifully with what she was wearing. My mum would never leave the house without having a quick cup of coffee and putting on her lipstick. Neither of my parents ever owned a pair of jeans.

Having older parents made me determined to never be an old mum. I was going to find my soulmate early, not wait and have to settle in a last-ditch attempt to have children. My soulmate and I would do exciting things, have amazing holidays and vibrant social lives. Then, when our perfect world couldn't get any better, we'd get married and have children. Besides, kids with older parents were always so 'square'. Back in the day, this meant goody-two-shoes children, who always followed the rules, and the term was used as an insult by the cool kids. This was something my sister and I agreed early on, would never happen to our children, since we'd be young, cool mums and our kids would be normal and fit in. I decided that my 20's was perfect timing and did not see any flaws in this plan. The plan was archived until the appropriate time had arrived.

As a teenager I was still very drawn to babies, when one of my many, many second cousins had a child, I'd be in there, wanting to hold the baby. I couldn't tear my eyes away, watching the little fists clamp and unclamp, loving when they would hold onto your finger so tightly. The softness of the skin on their tiny little fingers, and little cheeks. The ever so soft wispy hair, that smells amazing. The tiny, curly little toes. I loved the way their chubby little hands just popped out of their arms with seemingly no wrists and the same with their feet, with no noticeable ankles. The happy gurgles and smiles. Even the heart-breaking cries. When the little bottom lip wobbles, the look of utter despair, the need for comfort. I was drawn to everything about these little beings. I loved holding them, feeling a little baby in your arms just felt so natural, so amazing. I just simply loved babies. I remember a second cousin having twins when I was 16 and asking her loads of questions about having two at once. My mum took a picture of me cradling one of them, a picture I loved and pinned up on my cork noticeboard at the time. This would be me. Soon.

When we had to do a week of work experience at school, I went to a local nursery, where the children were all about three-four years old. At the time it was more through lack of inspiration than an active career choice. However, I loved spending time with the young children. I loved how they viewed things, their enthusiasm for the task in hand, the joy of just running around. I loved it when they would come to me because they were upset or had hurt themselves. I was just happy being around them. On my last day at the nursery, I had been asked to read the story at the end of both the morning and afternoon sessions. I was so sad leaving that day, I loved spending time with these little children. I really couldn't wait to have my own.

I met Soulmate #1 (because there is never just one), at University. He was The One, my all, my best friend. My parents had moved abroad at the same time I finished school, as had always been the plan. They moved to England at the start of their marriage on the understanding that after my dad retired, they would return to Switzerland. At the time, my sister was also living abroad, so Soulmate #1 also became my family.

I had started Essex University in 1996, after a year out, moving to Switzerland with my parents. I spent one term at Geneva University, studying International Relations. I hadn't really known what I wanted to study, or what I wanted to do after Uni, but thought this sounded interesting. It wasn't. Or at least I couldn't get into it. I also really missed England and my friends. Uni in Geneva is different, there is no campus, no student union (SU) bar. People go to their local university, so live at home and maintain the same friendship groups from school. I applied to come back to Uni in England, this time to study Molecular Biology, also simply because I was interested, rather than having a career goal. Turns out, this really was interesting. I loved Uni, the freedom of it, the social life. I always found it easy to make friends and soon had a great group of friends with whom I am still close today. I loved how I didn't need to make plans with anyone, at any given time, day or night, I could walk into the SU bar and find someone I knew well enough to have a drink with. In the days before mobile phones, meeting friends could be a logistical nightmare, so this was a real positive.

After Uni, Soulmate #1 and I got jobs and began the process of becoming responsible grown-ups, renting for a few years, then buying our first home. Life was fun, we had a great group of mates who lived locally. I'm not sure when I went from simply knowing I wanted children to wanting children RIGHT NOW, but I remember trying to be 'chilled' about it for a long time and not be a nightmare girlfriend with high demands. It was going to happen. We'd get married and then I'd be a mum. But I really wanted to be a mum now. I also remember feeling a bit embarrassed about it and trying my best to deny my own wishes. The little inner feminist was appalled that I would give up forging my career before having children, but it's all I really wanted. I had no clue what fabulous career I was going to have anyway. I fell into one job after another, only moving on because either I'd moved towns, I was bored, or I needed more money.

Straight after Uni I'd started working for an Insurance company, which was based locally, as we'd remained in Essex. Then, when we moved to London, I found a job there at an Estate Agents. I really didn't enjoy that role, so moved to the sales department of a Publishing firm, but the money there wasn't great so then I got a job in a Bank. There was no obvious career trajectory in any of my choices and I had no ambition in any of the roles I did have.

My dad died when I was 25, after falling ill with a brain tumour whist I was still at Uni. They had prepared us for the worst then, but he fought on for as long as he could. My relationship with him had always been quite fraught, from quite an early age and his death hit me hard. I hadn't made my peace, there was so much left unsaid, un-done. I had always thought our relationship would be mended when I had children, because although he struggled with close relationships, he was good fun and great at playing games which didn't require closeness. I felt his being a great grandad to my children would make up for our lack of relationship and we would be friends again.

However, I gave myself no time to grieve for him, just pushed on with life. I think because it had happened abroad and I flew back home straight after the funeral, it was easy to pretend nothing had changed, but a piece of my heart had broken and I did nothing to repair it at the time. I was all about where I was heading – marriage and babies. I was in my mid-20's, surely just fast-tracking now. I'd put a lot of effort into this destination. One by one my friends were getting engaged and then married. The natural next step was going to be babies. It was going to be me soon. Very soon. Just a bit more waiting. Maybe drop a hint....... Not this year then. Ok, no problem, another hint. I tried to keep my emotions in check, but this became more difficult as time went on.

Then the babies actually started appearing amongst our friends. I remember the first baby to really enter our lives as a couple, in 2003 one of our mutual friends from Uni had a little girl and my boyfriend had bought her a book, which he had found cute, about a fluffy owl. My heart melted. I knew he was on the same page as me. My turn was coming up. I hinted, strongly. And yet still I waited. As I headed into my late twenties, there was still no sign of marriage or babies. I did become more demanding with time and unfortunately, the relationship ended one month before my 29th birthday. We were not in the same place and definitely not headed in the same direction. He knew I would resent him for making me wait longer and he would resent me, if he gave in to keep me happy. He was wise and he let me go.

The physical pain of my broken heart was intense. I didn't know what to do with myself. I paced the flat and then I would crumble to the floor and sob. My soulmate was gone. My future erased. The One had walked away and left a huge, cavernous hole in his place, which nothing I tried could fill. I took much, much longer to let him go and even longer to realise his reasons were sound. My heart shattered and my life disintegrated around me. I didn't know how to be without him. He had been my all for so many years. I felt such a huge sense of rejection, of everything I was and everything I could be. I had not been enough. I didn't understand why we couldn't be together and make it work. Surely love was enough? As it turns out, no, it isn't.

Since my parents and sister lived abroad, I had moved to where his family and his friends lived in South East London. I suddenly found myself cast aside, feeling like I was in a tiny rowboat in the middle of the sea, with no horizon in sight, with no idea of which direction to row in. I had no one locally who was there for me. I tried briefly seeing his friends, who had become my friends over the years, but they were mostly single young men and had grown up with him, it wasn't a support network which worked. And seeing them was just a reminder of what I had lost, I couldn't do it. We sold our home and I reluctantly moved into my own tiny flat.

I stayed in South East London, but moved across one borough. It was easier to visit properties locally before or after work and I don't' think I had the space or calm in my mind to think about moving somewhere else and what that would mean about getting to work etc. South East London had become my home over the last few years. During my more feminist teenage years, this had been a dream of mine, having my own place. A little part of me was super proud of myself, going it alone, where I now knew nobody, a mighty pat on the back to me.

I found that along with my own heartache and my own judgement on myself, for having failed this relationship, there were the odd comments of judgement, which were really not meant harshly, people don't know what to say to someone in the throes of heartache. But all of it led me to have even less confidence in myself being a lovable person. Even articles seemed to point the finger at me, unable to 'hold onto' a man. I should have done this, not done that, worn this, said that.... He had chosen to end the relationship and yet according to all the Women's magazines, the responsibility of its termination seemed to sit entirely at my feet.

I remember one friend commenting that I hadn't tried hard enough to keep my boyfriend. I wasn't sure what to think of that? I didn't want to be with someone who didn't want to be with me. Even my mum, who should have been 100% on my team, was telling me what I could have done differently, things I needed to improve in myself, to make myself more loveable. My confidence was as low as it could get. I was already feeling so rejected and couldn't help but take these comments and articles to heart, more things I'd done wrong.

When you are suddenly alone after a long-term relationship ends, there is so much you seem to have to re-learn through the lens of a broken heart. How to breathe. How to wake up every day with the weight of your heart so heavy you have to 'coach' yourself out from under the duvet. How to function normally when you are numb and stuck in a dark fog of loss. How to go to a wedding, the ultimate celebration of love, and smile with genuine hope for the couple, when your very core has been betrayed by love. How to watch telly with no one to pass comment to. You realise how precious a sense, touch is. No hugs, no kisses, no physical closeness to another human, sleeping beside you, eating opposite you, no passing someone in the hall, no face you know every single line of, no physical contact of any sort.

My work social life became hectic. I was working in a sales department for a publishing firm based in North London at this time. It was a young and dynamic team and felt like an extension of Uni. We were all good friends and used to go to the local Walkabout pub, get drunk and dance the night away. We would often then travel into Central London to a club. I always had a keen internal homing pigeon, a part of me that knew, no matter how drunk I was, that now was the time to head home. I would suddenly stop dancing, I'd always pick up my coat and bags and exit quietly. Often I would not remember leaving or the journey home, but the pigeon always got me there. I'd wake to many texts asking where I'd got to and if I was ok? In hindsight this was quite reckless behaviour.

I was barely ever at home during the week, and instead I was propping up busy bars and dancing during the week, but weekends were awful, this is when everyone did things as a couple and, by now, as a family. I could easily leave work friends in a club on a Friday night and not see another living soul until my journey to work on Monday morning. My close friends didn't live nearby, I was alone and lonely. Loneliness is not just about being alone, because I do actually like my own company and can always find plenty of things to do.

Loneliness is when you know, no matter what, that no one can be there for you, whether that be physically or emotionally. This was demonstrated when I was in a serious car accident, my car rolled. I remember time slowing down, as I watched the tall Canary Wharf buildings in front of me become horizontal. It's a very surreal sensation. When I was in the ambulance, a policewoman came to ask if there was anyone they could call. There was not. Everyone who loved me was far away and had their own lives, partners, children and could not come at the drop of a hat, just to see me. This was one of my loneliest moments. I felt outside of society.

I spent a long time heartbroken after the loss of soulmate #1, trying to be ok, whilst all the time my biological clock (the one counting down my remaining fertility), which had been ticking pretty loudly, for some years now, had reached deafening proportions. Finding Soulmate #2 however, seemed to elude me. I was 29 when we split up and, being still single a couple of years later, I started thinking of a worst-case scenario plan. I knew that I did still want a relationship, but I was unwilling to compromise just to have a family. I would not settle for less than a soulmate and they don't come around so often. I remember after yet another awful date, one friend telling me to just put up with him, "surely he couldn't be THAT bad?" Then I would have someone to have a child with. I couldn't. It felt like a betrayal to myself, to what I wanted from a relationship. I wanted our love to be something in itself, not a means to an end.

I'd had so many disastrous dates, some of which really were quite comical, I was thinking of writing a book about them. But part of me was starting to despair on finding The One. I'd not expected it to take so long or be so difficult. I may be no oil painting, but I wasn't offensive looking either and I was good fun, pretty clever and usually easy going, these traits had stood me well in my younger years. Now I had the added bonus that I could hold my own in a drinking competition. What a catch!

I was just the wrong age. Any guys my age who were ready to settle down, already had. Guys who hadn't settled down, weren't intending to just now. I wasn't keen on looking for anyone much older, or younger. I felt there was no age-limit for me to find love, but having a child came with a very obvious sell-by date. Clearly, I needed a plan B. My clock could wait no more.

So, I started thinking about options, such as adoption, which was my initial thought, but also IVF, which I felt very uncertain of. I didn't know anyone who had been through it personally. I felt that it was not fair to willingly bring a child into the world knowing from the start that they wouldn't have two parents. I needed to find out more. All the while assuming that none of this would be necessary, I would find my soulmate, I was just being extra prepared. This was precautionary; in case it was needed. So, in 2007, at the age of 31, I started my five-year plan. In five years' time, less if at all possible, I would be a mum. I desperately saved money to get myself a home with two bedrooms and a little garden. Then I would have my child. Easy. It just needed a bit of time and hopefully a pay rise. I investigated what help was available in terms of financial support for single mothers, maternity leave, childcare vouchers at work etc. I was worried I'd not be able to do it.

On one particularly dark day, I had dared to wonder what if? What if I don't find anyone? What if I never have children? I would just live and then die. Unnoticed. How could I make my life mean something? I wanted to leave a small imprint of my existence onto life. It's then that I realised I wanted to help others, I wanted to be able to make a positive difference in people's lives. Not drift through life without leaving at least a footprint on someone's life. This is when I decided I would become a Psychologist. My grandma had told me when I was still a child that I had a good intuition about people, I could empathise with their situations. I've always tried to understand why people react as they do, how they feel and what made them feel that.

My initial thought was a Clinical Psychologist. So, whilst I was embarking on my five-year life plan, I also decided to throw myself into studying for a Psychology degree, through the Open University. It was tough alongside full-time work, but it gave me a focus and I felt this was the career I wanted to follow. I also decided to start volunteering at Childline, a charity set up so children can call for support, comfort and emergency help, if needed. I loved it there, although it was tough going. Every Monday night after work I'd go to Folgate Street, just opposite Liverpool Street Station where they were based at the time and do the 6pm-10pm shift. I'd get home at about 11pm, exhausted and often saddened by what I'd heard, but I hoped that I'd made a difference to someone. It also meant one less evening sat home alone, one less dinner-for-one.

In February 2008, I celebrated my 32nd birthday and moved jobs, from the publishing firm in North London, to a retail Bank in Central London, with a hope that I could speed up my saving. I moved from working in a buzzy sales department to the IT department. I had no knowledge of IT, other than owning a laptop and struggling with what was still dial-up internet at the time. This job however, was based in London Bridge, a much easier commute from South East London. I felt like I was taking positive steps for my future. I had a plan and was actively making it happen.

The bungalow

I have always loved being outside. My flat had only a tiny patch of communal grass, so when it was really sunny, I'd grab my books and a blanket and go and study in Greenwich Park. I loved walking up, through Blackheath. It's a lovely little corner of London, which feels like a village. It is a very fancy place to live and was full of young families, proudly pushing their offspring around the quaint little shops and restaurants. It was a beautiful scene of normal life. A scene I felt so left out of.

The park was worse, babies laughing, running, crying. Mums, dads, siblings, grandparents, ball games, picnics. Life. I felt that I was just observing life through a window. Like the Little Match Girl story I'd read years ago, who looked in on people's marvellous Christmas feasts, which she could almost taste in her mouth, but had no chance of eating, or feeling the warmth of. I could observe life, but this only made me feel how far away it was. I would sink into a sense of despair.

My natural state is a happy one, so I would always fight to get back to my normal self. Being so down did not feel natural to me and I would find my hope would bounce back, but it was harder, it took longer and was more of an effort to get back to me. I think this often made it worse, I would beat myself up for not being able to cheer up and not bouncing back so quickly. I couldn't get normal life right, find a partner, have children, I couldn't even get cheering up right. It became a bit of a vicious circle, something else I could hold against me. Still, it was summer, the season of love, let's take a look at which ever dating site I was on at the time....

As I worked on my five-year plan, my relationship with my mum was changing quite drastically. She had always been my rock during all my difficult times, but she had changed, or we had changed. So slowly, I didn't notice at first. I couldn't talk to her in the same way, she felt distant. She was eventually diagnosed as having a form of dementia and depression. I went through a period of grieving for the mum I'd had and the relationship we'd had. We had been very close, and I felt like I'd lost her already, even though she was still there. I could count my mum amongst my best friends. Now I no longer called her when I needed a chat, because I didn't want to burden her with my stories. I found our conversations were different, more circular, I didn't feel that my mum was there. This made me realise how desperately I wanted that closeness, that bond that we had shared and that I missed desperately.

I wanted to continue what we'd had, what she had also had with my grandma. I realised, I wanted to have my own biological child, in the hope of also preserving elements of my precious mum. There was no longer any question, I was going to have a child with the help of a sperm donor.

I had started a diary when I first decided that I was now working towards single motherhood, so that when I eventually had my baby, they would hopefully be able to understand why I had chosen this path and know that it was not a spur of the moment decision. I kept articles about fertility, which I also stuck into this diary, to show what was influencing my thinking, including one which stated that by the age of 30, women only had 12% of their eggs left. If ever there was something to scare me into taking action, this was it. I questioned every decision I was making. Was I being selfish? I needed to be sure my need to be a mother, my need for a baby wasn't more important than the feelings of any child I would have. They should be my priority. I loved them already, my babies, I had to do the right thing by them, even if that meant not have them.

22nd March 2009

Today is Mother's Day. The last few years I've started to feel awful as the cards start appearing in the shops, the teddy-bears, the mugs, feeling so far away from ever taking part in this day. Now I feel so much closer to it, knowing you are going to happen. Being a mum is so important to me. I love my mum so much; she is so amazing, and life would be bare without her. I want to share that with you. My mum has endless time for me and made my childhood magical. I'd like the opportunity of giving some of that back.

I did so much research, reading books and articles by women who had been through this, and by children conceived this way. I also read books by single mums and research on emotional impacts of being a child of fertility treatment but also a child in a single parent family. I wanted to know if it was fair on my child. I was concerned that I didn't have my dad around anymore to be a positive masculine figure. I read research papers on the psychological impact on children. I spoke to my friends, I would need my male friends on hand, to provide positive male role models. They were all amazing and very supportive.

One of my friends told me I was thinking about it way too much, that no parent asks themselves if they are being fair to their child, they just get pregnant. They just deal with whatever questions come up as and when they do. I felt that by making it a conscious choice to not have the perfect 'nuclear' family, it wouldn't be fair to not consider how the child might feel. I remember telling my mum when I was young, during the heat of an argument, that I'd never asked to be born. I guess that might be quite a common teenage outburst. Maybe I was over-thinking it?

I saved what I could, whilst still socialising a lot, partly enjoying new work friendships, partly avoidance of my empty flat, but also I still really wanted to meet someone and online dating wasn't working out well. I was also a little embarrassed I needed online dating at all, when everyone around me just met their partners in a normal way. I wanted a relationship, I wanted it all. The dream, the romance, the love, the marriage and my family. I knew that in terms of fertility I was now on the downward slope, the moment was now, but inside I still felt so young, I still loved going dancing, I wanted to believe Soulmate #2 was just the next night out away. I still hoped Plan B wouldn't be necessary. It would get pushed back to when absolutely necessary.

I celebrated my 34th birthday in 2010, I was now two and a half years into my 5-year plan and had mainly stuck to saving and research, no real action except for a new car. Since I worked with a large and varied team, some of my friends were considerably younger, which I think made me feel younger. I tried to bury myself in socialising, to not notice the passage of time. I think I fooled most people, including myself at times. Other times, I felt my dream drifting, whilst not wanting to admit this reality. I was outgoing and sociable and had many friends, I wasn't someone who would end up single. I would have the dream romance and family, that's the sort of life I was meant to have. However, the longer I was single, the more I started to believe that my path to motherhood would need to be under my own steam. I think such a big decision took me a while to accept. It felt like admitting defeat, that I'd not have a relationship, which I didn't want to believe.

27th March 2010

For the last few weeks, I've thought of nothing but you. Whether I'm doing the right thing or if I'm just thinking of me? I love you so much already! I think about what we'll do when we're together, about Easter, Christmas, the park, the magical moments I had as a child that I want to share with you. I can't wait to hold your hand. To read you stories, to have fun baths and watch you splashing and playing. I can't wait even for when you cry at night and I can come and soothe you. I hate night time too, it's when I feel the most lonely.

I can't wait to hold you, to love you, to see you smile. The two things which scare me most in all this are feeling isolated and not having enough money. I won't have a lot of support around here and if I'm not at work, I won't have a lot of adult conversation. I don't have a mum or anyone really who I can rely on to babysit around here, or to share in the joy of you. BUT, I will have you, my perfect little treasure.

All around me, families continued to be forming. I would send the new baby gift, go and visit, attend first birthday parties, feeling more and more distant from these seemingly normal activities. I used to love going to get little gifts for their births, cute babygrow's, blankets, towels, cute everything. I was looking forward to when I could buy these for my children. A couple of times the gift was so cute, I debated whether to keep that for my child and go and buy another gift for the baby. I never did, I didn't want to tempt fate, not that I ever believed in fate. I couldn't wait to get the congratulations cards myself. However, these things became progressively more difficult to do. I saw some cards for grandparents too, I thought about how much that would mean to my mum, to receive a card congratulating her on having grandchildren. I felt so much guilt and sadness for her, for the relationship I no longer thought she would have with my children. One like I'd had with my grandma.

I would meet with friends and their young families, it seemed so natural and made me wonder all the more, why no one wanted to have a family with me? It was so conflicting, I loved meeting with friends, but my heart would always break a little. I would usually cry on my journey home, dreading getting back to the empty flat, hating the fact that I was alone, feeling entirely unlovable. What was so wrong with me? I was starting to physically feel the absence of my baby. My arms felt empty, my uterus too. I had already waited so long, I had hoped to be close to having children when I was 24. Here I was 34 years old and no closer. I longed to hold a little baby of my own. My heart was filled with love for my unborn child. My uterus would spring to life whenever I saw a baby, it felt like it was doing an excited backflip, but it was filled with yearning. It wasn't a nice feeling, it always left me feeling extremely sad.

At 35, although I was still hopeful that I'd find a soulmate, I knew that fertility was not an endless stream of opportunities, so I thought there was no harm in getting the ball rolling on the last step of the plan. Finding The One was proving quite a challenge. I had given it a pretty good shot by anyone's standards. I hadn't sat back and waited. I had gone on every friend set-up, I had joined various sites, chatted to countless men online and by then I was into the 30+ first dates. Second dates were rare though and of those dates, only one gentleman made it to 3 dates. Even though I was not interested in any of these dates, I always felt that somehow I was to blame and I was at fault.

I had also been speed dating several times, which most of my married friends seemed to think sounded like a great night out. It truly isn't. My experience of it was quite demoralising. I struggled to find people I could hold a decent conversation with or felt a connection to. Or found remotely attractive. That said, I did have a short relationship with a very lovely gentleman I had met speed dating, back in 2007. He was perfect on paper, but my heart was still not healed when I had met him and I couldn't pretend. Soulmate #1 had left a hole in my heart that at the time I felt only he could fill.

I was often accused of being fussy, potentially fuelling my fear that it was somehow my fault I hadn't found anyone. I genuinely don't think I was. I didn't have a particular 'type' I was open to talking to anyone, but I was unwilling to settle for just someone. I was no shrinking violet, I was out a lot, I talked to a lot of people. I began to feel very discouraged about dating and finding a person I could really connect with. I needed to prioritise motherhood now. I remember a friend, a couple of years younger than me, telling me on a drunken night out, not to do it alone, only to be told a short time later that she was pregnant, because time wasn't on her side. I couldn't keep becoming a mum on standby any longer. Romance would have to wait.

In summer 2011, I plucked up the courage to go and speak to my doctor about how to go about IVF using a sperm donor. My doctor, a late middle-aged gentleman asked me if I didn't like men? It felt like a slap in the face. After all the attempts I'd made to find someone this was such a cruel judgement. I was single through no choice of my own. I already felt that I had botched up what everyone else seems to manage just fine. To find someone to love them enough to stay with them. I was already admitting what felt like failure to me, I was having to move to Plan B. I was scared about the journey I was undertaking, with no one to really share it with me. It was a massive unknown. I had no idea what to expect.

The insensitivity of this comment really stung. I felt tears threaten in my eyes, but managed to style them out, pretending I was fine. I had tried so hard to find a soulmate, they're just not that prevalent. I didn't want this. I wanted the dream, a husband who loved me, a family, the conventional way. That thoughtless, off-the-cuff comment hit way more nerves than this doctor would have known how to deal with. I was angry at his judgement and at myself for my failure. The doctor said I'd need a blood test and a referral, and that he would let his colleague deal with me, since she was the fertility expert in the practice. He didn't need to be an expert; he was referring me to a fertility clinic. I needed a referral letter. It didn't feel like that would be difficult to write. I felt like he was just pushing me to another doctor, an embarrassing case he did not want to deal with. A poor, lonely woman who couldn't find herself a man. He seemed to want no part in my twisted journey to motherhood. I went away crushed and ashamed.

I was very open to my friends about my plans, I had discussed this with some work friends too. My mum was always very open and honest with us and I've inherited this trait. I actually feel like I'm lying to someone if I don't tell them the truth, even if sometimes I'd rather keep something to myself, it still just comes out, before I'm even ready for it to. Nearly everyone around me was in a couple, having or had already had children, it felt good to feel like I was catching up with the crowd at last.

When I went to see the fertility expert at the same clinic, it was very different. This doctor was lovely and so considerate. She would refer me to Kings Fertility Unit but I had to have a blood test first. I had to wait for day one and then day 21 of my next period. When you start something like this, waiting is hard. I had waited longer than I had wanted already to have children, in the hope I wouldn't need to do it alone, so prolonging that wait further felt like torture. When you're waiting for your periods, the days and weeks feel very long.

18th September 2011

I had my second lot of blood tests a week ago now and get the results on Wednesday. I'm really scared of what the outcome will be. Have I left this too late? I feel lonely to not share this anxiety with anyone.

I'm so excited about finally being a mum. Finally finding my place in the world. I cannot bear the idea it won't happen. I'm trying to keep my mind off

Wednesday. I feel so happy that soon you'll be part of my life. We'll begin our little family together, our own little adventure story. I'm so excited to get to know you!

The blood tests came back fine, nothing to report. I was fine to go ahead with any fertility treatment, she sent the referral and I just needed to wait to hear back from the clinic.

My five-year plan, was now down to its final year and no baby in sight still, but it felt close. I had put my flat on the market earlier in 2011. I started looking locally for a two-bed place with a garden. I had considered moving back to where I'd grown up in Berkshire and my school friends all lived, but it turned out I couldn't afford it. I'd have to pay roughly the same in-house prices, but my commute to London would cost three times as much. My journey would also be longer. One of my friends there offered to look after my baby whilst I was at work. That felt amazing, just the fact this child existed in other people's thoughts. Unfortunately, since work would be further away, I'd have to leave my child for more hours a day, which did not feel right. I was having a child to spend time with them. It was not worth it unless I could get a local job. A new job meant I'd likely only get statutory maternity pay. Besides, that sort of move takes time and co-ordination, which I didn't feel I had the time to do. I needed to get this plan underway. My salary was good, I'd not be so lucky in a local job. I decided as a single mum, I had to play it safe and stay with the decent salary, shorter commute and good maternity leave.

I had found a cute place in the summer of 2011. A bit small, but with quite a big kitchen, where I could imagine my child doing their homework on our big dining table. An odd dream, considering I rarely did homework, I even ended up having some Friday night detentions because of my lack of homework. These were usually reserved for the most rebellious pupils, in our quiet little school. I don't remember my parents ever really asking if I had any homework or if I'd done it. Perhaps because of this, it became important for me, I wanted to know if my kids had homework and to help them with it. The kitchen table was the perfect spot, whilst I prepared dinner. This kitchen would do.

This cute little place was the house where I would live with my beautiful family. I put in an offer and they accepted. Wow, step two of my five-year plan ticked. My flat however was not doing so well. I received a couple of very low offers. Not enough. Then, when I had an interested party, the sellers of my new house pulled out, they had decided to no longer sell, after having accepted my offer a few months ago. I was back to square one, this was a blow to the plan. I briefly considered shelving it all and going to work with Orangutans in Borneo for a year. I felt so betrayed by life. I just wanted a family, I was tired of fighting, but the deafening clock just wouldn't let up. So, I continued with more viewings.

The estate agent was desperate to show me a bungalow they had on their books. It had been on the market for a long time. I assumed they were desperate to get rid and since I wasn't 80 years old, I kept saying no. After an umpteenth visit to a disappointingly small terraced matchbox, the agent said she happened to have the keys to the bungalow, and she thought I really ought to view it. I went to see it, reluctantly, but we were out, and she'd driven, so may as well. It was HUGE. The garden was a real garden, not a postage stamp. All that space. It had a second bedroom, really very small, but big enough for a cot and that's all I needed right now, but the kitchen, living room and garden were bigger than in all of the other houses I'd visited. The offer was made and accepted in November 2011.

I had found the perfect place to start my family. The plan was back on. I set about preparing to move. I love moving to a new house. Its cleansing and usually is an improvement from the previous place. This move was very exciting. Not only was my new living room the size of my entire flat currently, but I had the massive garden. Outdoor space of my very own. How I had missed this. Mixed with excitement, I was also filled with dread, I was terrified I'd overshot this, buying this place by myself, was I about to bankrupt myself? Emotions on the run up to the move were very split, during the day I was filled with excitement and dreams of what was to come, at night I would feel my whole head tingle with fear about having taken on too big a financial burden, the tingling felt so intense at times, I feared I'd wake up bald! Daylight again and I would think this home was where I would bring my new baby home. I would make it work. We would have such adventures together. This was the start of my family and I couldn't wait.

Christmas that year felt positive. I went to Geneva to be with my mum, sister and extended family as I did every year. I had my new home, pictures of which I bought to show my family. In Switzerland people don't buy so much, they tend to have long-term rentals. So, me, buying my own little house was quite a thing. I glowed with pride, see, I could 'do' life too. I was so positive that New Year, 2012 was going to be MY YEAR! My luck would change, things would fall into place this year, I knew it. In February 2012 I moved into my beautiful little bungalow. The day I got my keys I went in and ran around the living room, this was it!.

24th February 2012

Well here we are, home. Unpacked. This place is amazing. I can't wait to hear you running around it, squeals of joy as you run around the garden. It has a really long hallway and I can imagine your little feet running along it. One step closer to you!

I've been trying so hard to find someone to share my life with, so that you have a daddy too, it just isn't that easy. I so want you to have the best life and feel so guilty that I might not provide that for you.

I hope you will understand why I couldn't just keep waiting to find a dad, you mean so much to me, being a mum means so much. I am old in the motherhood stakes. I can't let this joy slip through my fingers just because the universe can't arrange a decent date! It sounds so selfish when I say it that way, all about me. I guess it is really. I need to have you in my life. I need to be a mum. I do think its ingrained though, its part of survival of the species, we have to want to have children and for me, this is too strong a need to fight, I do genuinely feel like my life depends on it.

Matilda

I was now 36 and STILL single, 0 cigarettes, a bit too much wine, actually no idea on my weight. Bridget Jones eat your heart out. I was still going on dates, most of which, felt like hours I would never get back and therefore, I was now being a little more choosy, with whom I was willing to spend those hours.

My opinion when I started online dating was that the more people you meet, the better. It's a numbers game. I had read an article about the amount of single people being higher in London and New York, because many people there are just enjoying single City life. I also read an equation about the likelihood of finding a soulmate. In a population the size of London, there were two men which would be a perfect match for me. Two. I have since read another equation where there may be around 800. Still a bit of a needle in a haystack in a population of well over 8 million. However, now I felt that the downside of my numbers game was the demoralising reality that there are a lot of numpties out there. This truth had started to outweigh the statistical benefit.

Some friends of mine had created a profile for me on mysinglefriend.com and we would have drunken nights scrolling through profiles whilst they liked some cute guys on my behalf. Embarrassingly I rarely heard back from any of them, but every now and then I'd get a 'like' from a gentleman of around 60 years old. I started worrying that this was now the level I needed to peg my hopes on. It really didn't do much for my confidence.

In March 2012, I had, after five years studying in the evenings and weekends, passed my Psychology degree. I was proud of me. It had been tough going, work had not offered any support in the form of study leave. I would take annual leave a week before my exams, then cram my revision that week. I wanted to go into Clinical Psychology, which needed a masters and doctorate, both of which were expensive. The masters would need to be two years, since I couldn't afford to work part time. Even over two years, I may have to work a condensed week. I wasn't sure how I could make that work with a baby. As for the doctorate, I'd need to get sponsorship via the NHS. I'd therefore have to leave my job, my salary would be less, I assumed any maternity support would be impossible. It all felt completely at odds with my priority which was a family.

I met a Clinical Psychologist on a night out and discussed the role with him, he told me that he doesn't get to chart the progress of clients like you would as a therapist, working with them and able to see their ongoing development. He mostly did assessments and passed clients on to others for therapy. That's not what I wanted. One of the things I struggled with at Childline was that it was usually a one-off conversation, you don't get to know how someone gets on, or support them any further (although there are some regular callers). I decided Clinical Psychology was not for me, Psychotherapy was. I researched what I needed in order to become one of those and signed up to the local Adult Education College, to start evening classes that Autumn.

It had been several months since my blood tests, and the referral letter from my doctors surgery, and I finally received a letter confirming my first appointment at Kings College Hospital, in South London. At the time, I'd been busy finishing my degree and moving house, so the timing worked out well. In hindsight I'm annoyed that I had to wait the normal NHS waiting time, when this was private treatment, it just happened to be taking place at an NHS clinic. Regardless, the date was set. This was real now. I was doing it. Alone.

I started thinking more about the day to day realities of becoming a mum. What our life would be like? What I would be like as a mum? How would I discipline? How would I deal with a temper tantrum in the supermarket? What would I do when I had to work again, full time, but my child was still not sleeping through the night? I really hoped I could afford to drop a day and only work a four-day week. I wondered what our holidays be like. I guessed we'd struggle financially but wondered whether I could pick up a cheap campervan, that way we could go on adventures. I started saving all the £2 coins I'd get, as a fund for my campervan. We would get by just fine; we would have each other. We'd be a little team.

I waited impatiently for the appointment date. I had a day out with a group of friends, husbands and children in tow. Such a wonderful day. The children were all growing up before my very eyes. I had so hoped that my children would play with them. I loved the way they all played with one another, like cousins. But the older they got, the less likely this seemed. As a child, my sister and I were really close to my older cousin. She was three years older than me, and 10 months older than my sister. Often, we played well together, but sometimes I would really feel how much younger I was, they wouldn't include me in games, or would try to scare me. I knew that too big an age difference meant that my child wouldn't be part of the group. It broke my heart, for my child to not have this relationship with the children of my closest friends. I didn't have nieces or nephews, my friends were the closest they would have to family and I'd managed to exclude them, and me, from this experience. I felt that familiar ache. I longed to be a family. More sobbing on the way home.

This was always such an emotional conflict, since, like seeing family, I always feel more like me again after spending time with close friends and yet I found it so difficult. It really emphasised what was missing in my life. I felt embarrassed that I had been unable to find a new boyfriend, when I had tried so hard to and still felt the weight of shame, that my soulmate had preferred a life without me in it. I missed the closeness of the relationship I had with Soulmate #1. He had felt like home and I still felt adrift. I felt like I didn't quite fit in anymore, I was too broken. I was starting to feel more and more like I was somehow separated by a pane of glass. An invisible separation and yet keeping me apart from the group. From society really. I felt like I was not involved in real life. I felt alone even in their company.

The day of my appointment arrived, and I went to the clinic with such trepidation. The fertility clinic was right at the back of the Kings Hospital campus. I walked for ages and still hadn't found it. I started to panic I'd be late. Of all the days. There was a security door, with a camera, both on the ground floor and on the first floor. This made me nervous. I walked in and gave my name. I sat down in an empty waiting room. I'd bought a book but couldn't read. What had I started? I saw little stars with names on the wall. Babies. Successful IVF. This was it, my future started now. I felt very emotional and excited suddenly and my eyes filled with tears. Then a couple came in and sat together, so I styled it out, tried to look like I was casually gazing out of the window. They looked anxious too and were holding hands tightly. Then another couple came in. I felt embarrassed to be there alone. Not good enough for anyone to love. My confidence took another knock.

I was called through to speak to the first consultant. He was cold, he knew his stuff, but I was not a person to him. He went through a lot of detail which felt like a foreign language. Various procedures I'd possibly need, drugs, the likelihood of decent eggs at my age and how that likelihood drops very dramatically over the next two-three years. A woman between 35-39 has a 25% chance of pregnancy every month, the traditional way, a woman of 40 has a 5% chance. He explained the percentage chances of successful IVF at my age or if I wait any longer. NHS success rates for women the age of 38-39 are 15%, this drops dramatically at the age of 40, to 9% success, although each clinic have their own figures related to their client base. Regardless, I really was cutting it fine now. I was kicking myself at having waited so long.

We also discussed what happens to any remaining embryos? Would I be happy to give any 'waste' to science? I then had to agree to pay close to £6,000 for a treatment which couples, including single-sex female couples, get free from the NHS through my Primary Care Trust. Another bitter pill to swallow about being single. Recently it's been in the news that the government recommendations are that any woman under the age of 42 receive three cycles via the NHS. Any woman. If only I'd known at the time, I might have been able to argue this.

I had a first internal scan, which was as much fun as it sounds. I was diagnosed with endometriosis, which could put into jeopardy my baby dreams. It had been left untreated for years, since its often managed using the contraceptive pill but due to severe migraines I'd had to stop taking the pill a decade earlier. I'd never really heard of endometriosis, certainly not paid any attention to it. The doctor treated me as if I was some kind of uneducated couth, asking if I had not realised that my periods were unusually painful? How could I know? How could I realise that what I felt during my periods wasn't how everyone felt? I was made to feel like I should have known. I should have had this treated since I wanted children. I had been irresponsible. The consultant told me that I may not be able to conceive at all, simply, matter-of-factly, coldly. As if this wasn't a huge blow.

He clearly did not know or care how long I have waited to have a child. I had waited too long. I think deep down, I just assumed at some point I would find someone, I would have our biological child. The idea that I might not be able to carry a child at all had never occurred to me. This was life changing news and I felt life changed. I felt winded! The tears threatened, but I used everything I had to hold them back. He, entirely oblivious, carried on talking about options. He seemed very happy to proceed with the cycle, I just needed to sign the forms. He didn't seem to be worried about having my endometriosis treated.

I was crushed on leaving this consultation. It was a tough day to process. Starting IVF alone is scary. Signing off £6,000 to the unknown is scary. Finding out that you may potentially not be able to do it at all was even scarier. I felt like I'd been hit in the stomach by an invisible wrecking ball. I hadn't seen it coming. I went back to my new, empty house, alone, scared, unsure and very deflated. I had no one to talk this through with. I had no one there to cheer me on. My own inner cheerleader really needed some work.

I got home and researched Endometriosis. It is a condition where tissue similar to the womb lining (endometrial tissue) grows outside the womb, around the body. It seems to mainly impact the ovaries and fallopian tubes, but it can travel well outside of this area. It develops abnormal bands of fibrous tissue which can cause pelvic tissue and other organs to stick to each other. It causes severe period pain and can cause sex to be painful. Since this endometrial tissue responds to the monthly hormone cycle, just as the lining of the uterus thickens then breaks down and bleeds every month, so does all the other endometrial tissue, regardless of where it is. The damage caused by it cannot be reversed. It can cause scarring, cysts and lead to fertility problems.

I read that surgical removal of the endometrial tissue is saved for the most severe cases. It can be permanently cured in 50% of these women, in the rest, symptoms can return within a year. Perhaps this is why the consultant was happy to go ahead with the treatment, maybe I wasn't a severe case. However he had also stated my fertility could be in question. I felt I needed to have another opinion about this.

Shortly after this appointment, I met someone. He was an old acquaintance who had recently split from his wife. Ironically after years of fertility treatment had taken its toll on their relationship. My first instinct was that this was far too soon for him, I was a rebound, but he managed to convince me this was not the case and since I was enjoying his company, I wanted to believe in the potential of us. I enjoyed the relationship and, I am ashamed to say, I actually started thinking perhaps this is how I have my baby. I thought I should be the loved-up girlfriend, in a hope that somehow this would make it real. I tried. I hoped. However, six months into the relationship, just before Christmas, he walked away.

Aside from the huge sense of rejection, and feeling used and betrayed, I was so, so disappointed. I had hoped this might be something. I had tried to make it more than it was. Most of all, I was furious that I'd wasted so much of my precious fertility, not pursuing a baby. I felt he had wasted my time; he knew my plan. I had stupidly put my treatment on hold all this time. For a guy. For the chance of the normal family created the conventional way. Never again! My need for motherhood was too great, my remaining fertile years too few.

Christmas, again. No closer to it being the magical family festival of my dreams, of my childhood. I had promised myself this time last year that everything would be different and here I was, starting another New Year, single and childless. 2012 had been year five of my five-year plan. The plan had been driving all my thoughts and actions and yet it still ended without me being a mum. This coming year would be different. 2013 was the year it would all happen. I willed the galaxy, the fairy dust, the magic, life, to see right by me. I was putting the positive energy in, making things happen, being proactive, everyone knows you get back what you put in. This year, I would get back all the efforts for the last few years.

For my 37th birthday, I got myself a cat. As with everything, this had not been a spur of the moment decision. I had decided I'd get a cat a few years back, but my flat was tiny, so I had to wait until I'd moved. My beautiful Matilda walked into my life and was the best friend I could have asked for. Having never owned a pet other than goldfish, I wasn't sure what to expect. I went to the shelter expecting to pick up one of the three kittens they had recently picked up, along with their mother. I went into the outdoor cage where these four cats were. A beautiful little black and white cat came over very curiously. She was very small, smaller than the other three. I found out this was the mother and she had not touched any food or moved for the 3 days she'd been there. I knew she was my cat. I think she knew I was her human. She came to me. The first night she slept in the living room. I think she did the second night also. After that she was on the bed and we were inseparable. Suddenly, where I had previously avoided coming home, instead, finding anyone willing to go for a quick drink, I found I couldn't wait to get home. Matilda felt the same, she would always be at the front door when I opened it and proceeded to run up and down the hall with excitement after I got home. I had found my little patch of heaven. It was my lovely new home and this magical cat. 2013 would be amazing!

12th March 2013

It's been a while since I've written to you. I've felt so upset and angry. I had met a guy, who I thought might be a good dad for you. I let myself believe, worse, I waited. I've lost so much time on hope, on believing life will work out as if by magic. I mean who is stupid enough to believe they could meet their other half and just start dating and that would be that, life would begin? I was that stupid. I feel like I let you down. I lost sight of having you, of our family.

You are my priority, the most important thing. I was hoping you would have a biological mum and dad. It would make things easier. You wouldn't need to read this diary for a start. You would have the traditional 'how we met' story from your parents, not a 'why I made you' story from a single mum.

However, I have got a surprise for you, I got Matilda, the best little cat in all the land. She is so cute; she loves a snooze on the bed. I can't wait for you two to meet. She's very gentle, I think she'd like to come and snooze with you. My heart melts thinking about it.

I saw another consultant who confirmed I had stage 4 endometriosis, the most severe. I would need an operation to remove all the growths and possibly some of my uterus lining. I was able to get this treatment privately through work, to avoid any long waiting lists. Although fertility treatment isn't permitted, since endometriosis can be quite debilitating in itself, it was on the list of acceptable procedures. The date was set for early June 2013. More waiting. I hated how aware I was of my fertility ebbing away. Every period felt like a wasted opportunity. I would cry every time a period started. It was no longer tears of PMT but of loss. I felt almost like I was mourning what could have been.

The consultant was amazing, he seemed to genuinely care. He knew why I was having the surgery. He warned me that removal of the endometrial tissue could cause scar tissue, which could then impact my ability to carry a child. My heart sank. Again. Carrying a child was the whole point of all this. I had to sign a disclaimer, by which I understood this could be a by-product of this surgery, as could damage to my internal organs and I could potentially require the permanent use of a colostomy bag. My desire to have a child was strong enough to make me just sign this disclaimer, regardless. Motherhood at any price!

This was my first ever general anaesthetic, I was terrified and very melodramatically, had emailed my sister, so she knew what to do, should I not come out of it. I got the bus up to the hospital. I was talked through the procedure and when the time came, wheeled to the pre-op room, where a couple of nurses got me ready. I was so scared, but kept thinking of the goal, my baby. Going under was so quick. Scary in being powerless, whilst at the same time quite liberating to let go. I came to in a nice sunny room and felt fine, although very sleepy. I dozed on and off for a while, with no real concept of time. I was bought some lunch and then got ready to leave.

A friend was picking me up and staying with me, until another friend could come over after work to stay with me overnight, since you're not supposed to be alone after a general. There was no set time, because I didn't know what time I'd be discharged. I was told I was ok to leave and I let my friend know. I needed to wait until after work. That was a couple of hours yet. Suddenly I felt overwhelmed, and panicky. Like now the surgery had happened and I was ok, I didn't need to be strong anymore. I just needed to get out of that room, out of that hospital, get home. I had a bit of a meltdown and suggested I get a taxi. My friend thankfully calmed me down and told me to just wait.

I think that's my way, I'm quite good in an emergency, I keep a cool head, but when it's done, when everything is safe, well it's open season to all the emotions. I was the same when my mum was taken to hospital for a suspected stroke. I was super calm, until we got the all-clear and we could go home. That's when I burst into tears. Also, when I crashed my car, I stayed in control through the ambulance journey, several X-rays and tests. Then I was discharged, I stumbled out of the hospital in a daze and cried the whole journey home in the cab. I had been terrified of having surgery and frightened about any complications which I'd had to sign away beforehand. But I was out, I was ok, I pulled myself together and waited.

I remember discussing IVF with my friend at the time. She always thought she'd be a mum, but she felt that she'd not want to do IVF, and said if she couldn't have children, then she'd just get a dog. I remember wondering what it is, that makes one woman willing to do absolutely anything it takes in order to achieve motherhood when others are happier to just accept whatever happens. Is it hormones? Is it upbringing? Is it your own relationship with your mum? It can't just be that. It must be biological. It would certainly be an interesting study. Maybe not so much for the women who are heartbroken at the time.

I think there is a lot of biology behind it, certainly for me. It's not just an emotional wish, or a want, like you would want marriage, or a fulfilling career. For me, it feels much deeper than that, more basic, like it's the very core of my existence. It feels as urgent a need as that of water, like my very being is compromised without it. I feel its absence like an essential part of me is missing. I hate the fact there is a biological deadline to motherhood, although the scientist within me understands it.

There have been studies done on why we have the menopause, it has been found to be useful for the survival of the species and of your genes in particular. If you are no longer burdened by the work of bearing children, then you are able to support your own children and grandchildren in bringing up theirs, therefore keeping your genes going. This phenomenon has also been seen in Whales and Elephants. To me however, the menopause is looming far too close and I hate it. I want to be burdened by bearing my children, desperately! I can't help my children and grandchildren with their children until I have mine first. I wish I could find the pause button on time.

A girl gets used to her periods being a certain way, it is very disconcerting when this changes. Following the surgery, what had been an excruciatingly painful few days of grimness, by this I mean, barely able to stand pain, that painkillers just didn't touch, with very thick, dark, almost black blood, turned into just some painful cramps with actual blood, red liquid blood and the whole thing was over in three days. Three days! This felt positively easy in comparison. How had I not known that I had endometriosis? I just assumed that what I experienced before was what periods were. I felt like the consultant's condemnation may have been well-placed. Now I could see the difference, it seemed obvious, I should have known. I could have had this treated years ago. This additional time wasted was on me.

I went back to see the consultant who had carried out the surgery. He told me the full extent of the endometrial growths. Seems there had been a lot of it, all around my innards. Both of my fallopian tubes had been tethered, so they couldn't move, which the doctor explained meant I would never have got pregnant, because the tubes are meant to move around fluidly. One of them had apparently been strangled and was now quite swollen, but that should ease up. He did say however that I was extremely lucky in that I had no endometrial growth inside my uterus. Therefore, they had not needed to do any surgery on the lining. What relief....no danger of scar tissue there. However, he did break it to me that I had a small fibroid on the outside of my uterus, but he felt it was small enough to not need to be removed, therefore avoiding further danger of scar tissue. However, a fibroid itself could impact the ability to carry a child to term. So not completely good news. He seemed really pleased with the surgery, considering the extent of the growths. He had also carried out a laparoscopy, going up into each fallopian tube to test whether they were blocked. They were clear. He didn't think there would be a problem conceiving now and, in vast contrast to the first GP I had seen, he wished me well with having my baby and gave me such a genuine smile, he meant it!

27th June 2013

My first surgery. Its quite a weird experience, knowing its actually quite dangerous, but the doctors and nurses are so used to it, they're very relaxed. I felt so vulnerable heading into surgery. I also didn't know the full extent of what needed to be removed. However I am very impressed with my scars. It was keyhole. All I have are three little crosses where they went in to look around and laser the growths. I don't think they'll show at all in a couple of years. Amazing technology!

I never thought I'd be having surgery just to have a baby. Its meant to just happen as a woman. Grow up......have babies. That's the deal. It's odd to think that without the surgery, I couldn't have had you. Even if I'd had someone here and we'd been trying naturally. Like when I was told I might not be able to carry a child at all at the clinic, the thought feels very alien. Still, I'm now one step closer, my baby.

I had to wait a while to heal after the surgery, before I could carry on with IVF. More waiting. More eggs lost every month. Over the summer, I had several BBQ's with various groups of friends. I felt like I was in a parallel world. I was still me; my friends were still themselves, but there was a barrier of sorts. I wasn't part of the same world anymore. I was filled with hurt and longing. I was so happy in their company and yet it made me feel so different, so apart, like I was an observer into their world of relationships and children, even their parents, with all the bustle; noise; joy; love; worry; hurt; stress; anger; but mostly, life, that this engendered. I felt like I was existing, not living.

Although my friends were supportive, I think many didn't really understand my need or my pain. I remember one friend would often ask if I wanted his children, when they were misbehaving or being difficult. Did he want the honest answer? To joke so casually about what was so painful for me made me feel even more separated from his world. A world where this was simply a light-hearted comment on how exhausting children can be. I wished I lived in that world, where this innocuous comment didn't dig like a knife.

I also remember another friend seeming to think I had a rosy image of what family life was and that I was lucky to not have the stresses of family life. Life is stressful. You hurt, you struggle, you lose people you love, you have arguments, you have financial worries, I understand that. I know a family doesn't remove those and, in some cases, adds to them. But they are part of life. The very essence of life. Without family then what is there? Just me. No one else to worry about, but also no one to talk to, no one to care about, no one to love. A weekend by yourself may sound like bliss when you never have a moments peace, but every single weekend alone, year after year, after year. Every evening alone, every bank holiday weekend alone, every birthday alone, every long drive home alone, every group event, alone, is pretty unimaginable to most. Family is so taken for granted by those who have it.

Finally, I was ready to begin. I called the clinic and was given a selection of six profiles of the donors on their books. Another option is to buy online, but obviously there could potentially be more risks with that. It was like online dating, with no pictures. It's all anonymous. However, each of them had written a letter for a potential child, which only the child would receive. Laws have changed and a child is able to contact their donor parent, but there is no expectation that the donor parent maintains contact.

I remember reading through each of them, over and over. There was eye colour, hair colour, height, weight and a list of interests. One stood out, he was tall, light brown hair, slim, sporty and seemed pretty clever, interested in reading and science. A geek like me! He felt right. I went into the stairwell at work to call the fertility clinic. The embryologist I spoke to was very kind, we discussed it, she mentioned that he only had another two years on their books, but that if I wanted more than one child, she would see if he may extend.

More waiting, another period came and went. Three weeks later, she called me back to say he would extend, for a further three years. I felt honoured he would do this for me. The embryologist then said that although I could not receive a copy of the letter, she could read it to me. I sat down as she read this. He explained why he was doing this, that he wanted to help people who could not conceive naturally but did not feel he wanted children of his own. He also said that when the time comes, if you (the child) want to meet and he was unable to, know that it is not because he wasn't interested or pleased, but that his life as it was, or the circumstances he found himself in, meant it wasn't right for him or his family at that time. It was funny, warm, so considered and kind that it made me cry. Right there, in the office stairwell, I knew I had chosen the right one. The father of my child. I felt so emotional, such a huge decision and I had to calmly walk back to my desk.

Next came more scans. I also needed to order the drugs separately, I was shocked at how expensive they were, close to £1,000 for a couple of months' worth of drugs. Considering these are created in bulk and probably cost a few pence each to produce, that seemed particularly expensive. I didn't have much money and was saving everything I could. In all the IVF treatment, this is what I resented paying for. I had to get it delivered to work and was concerned because one of the drugs needs to remain refrigerated, would it be ok until I got home? I really hoped no one would ask what this huge box was. At the time, everyone was having things delivered to work, it was common practice, until the post room put a stop to it, so it wasn't unusual and it would save the delivery arriving when I wasn't home.

Little Egg

So, off I went, starting the last leg of this journey. I had to wait for the next period to start, it was a long wait. First, I was put on the pill, so they knew where I was in my cycle. This seemed so counter intuitive. I wanted to have a baby not stop one, and this was wasting precious time. This was three weeks of treatment, but it was not optional. Next the mini menopause. I had to inject myself with drugs to induce a menopausal state to ensure they were starting at zero. Again, this seemed to go completely against what I was trying to achieve. I did however enjoy the hot flushes. As someone who never feels warm, unless it is at least 25 degrees, hot flushes in October was a relief. The other side of that coin were night sweats which were not pleasant.

6th October 2013

So much has happened since I last wrote, I don't know where to start. Yesterday I started the first lot of drugs to have you. I cried. I cried because it's terrifying to do this alone. I have never given up trying to have a family the traditional way, so you could be conceived in love, with two parents. I so wanted that for you. I have since found out that my sister has premature menopause and I was terrified I had waited too long, so I'm going ahead.

I was sent a list of six sperm donors to choose from. I didn't know how to make that choice? Which one sounded more like someone I might date? Which one sounded like a child I'd want? Which sounded like he'd make a good dad? How do you make a choice like that? I decided I wanted you to look as much like me as possible, so you could always recognise yourself in me and see where you came from. I hoped that at least you would have fair hair and blue eyes. I don't want you to feel like there's something missing. That sounds *ridiculous, of course you will, you will have so many questions.*

The donor I picked seemed clever, had varied interests in science, music and was sporty. He had light brown hair, the other five had dark hair. This seemed good. I was also allowed to hear a letter he wrote for you, which you will receive when you are 18. It was a beautiful letter.

I've been thinking about how we'll talk about your biological father. I don't know much about him other than that very short description of him and how I felt when I heard his letter in which he came across kind. How will you feel with my lack of information? Will you be angry? Will it be enough? I suspect when you're little it will be ok but after that? I really hope you can understand why I chose this.

I received all the drugs in one go, there is a terrifying amount of drugs, some of which I will need to inject myself with. It was expensive too, I'm so worried about how we'll cope. I'm angry that couples get this treatment for free, when nothing says that they can provide a better, more loving or more stable home. I have worked so hard to provide a beautiful and safe home for you.

As part of my treatment with the clinic, I had to see their counsellor. I had to see her once but could choose to see her again if I felt the need. I was actually looking forward to this visit to the clinic. This encounter would be friendly and non-judgemental. I met this lady, she seemed nice enough, but I didn't get a sense that she understood me nor that she wanted to try to. I looked at her hand, she was married. I remember thinking "you really don't care about me, but nice dress though". I talked; she signed a form. We never saw one another again.

Having now completed my counselling and psychotherapy training I know that this was not a counselling. I found myself wondering if she had ever even experienced infertility? Maybe she had, but with her husband and therefore my journey may not have felt like a valid one to her? She seemed entirely indifferent to a desire to have a child. I'll never know, but I do know I didn't leave the room with a warm feeling of empathy or a sense of having been heard or understood.

I then had to see a nurse, who showed me how to mix the drugs and inject myself. She mentioned I could get my partner to do this for me. Yeah, I'll just get home and ask him. I didn't say anything, just smiled. I was told to go either into the stomach or the thigh and to alternate sides every day. I started with my stomach, left side, right side. On the third evening I tried the left thigh. OH WOW! The pain! It burned. You can't undo an injection I just had to sit it out. Stomach it is then.

The final stage was stimulating egg production, again injecting myself. These had to be at the same time every day. Why on earth had I decided on evenings? At the time it made sense, I'm not a morning person, I can't really function until after a couple of coffees, neither of which I have time for at home before heading to work. Evenings these days I was usually at home. However, this meant that when I went to see a friends' daughters' ballet show one evening, I had to disappear into a friends' car for a few minutes to administer the shot. I hoped no one would notice me at this children's event, shooting up in the car park like a junkie.

25th October 2013

I took my last pill today. That's step one done. I also started the jabs today, first one 10 minutes ago, it still stings a bit. The pills gave me raging headaches and I've not slept well for the last three weeks; I wonder what effects the jabs will have? Still, you will be worth it. I'm so worried this won't work, it has to!

During my cycle, I had a series of appointments, scans, blood tests etc. I would go to the clinic, usually during my 'extended' lunch hour, since I had not told anyone in my team about this treatment, this meant I was running a lot. Kings was not an easy hospital to get to from work in London Bridge. I would then sit in the waiting room, watching couple after couple come in and leave together, highlighting my singleness. That used to sting each time. Making babies alone is a really lonely business! I have since had a friend undergoing IVF with her husband who told me I was truly brave to do it alone, as it is such a rollercoaster of emotions. I do not think I was brave, I never felt like it was a choice, I needed a baby, my life would not be complete until I was a mum, bravery didn't come into it, I just had to. Facing the loneliness was braver.

Each time I left the clinic I had more bad news it seemed. It was always emotional. It had started with having endometriosis and potentially not being able to carry a baby at all. Then I found out one of my ovaries had been detrimentally impacted by the endometriosis, so it was unlikely to produce any eggs. Less eggs to fertilise. The next time I went in for a scan, to see if I was ready to start the second lot of jabs, the scan showed there was liquid in my right Fallopian tube. The consultant told me that this would reduce my chances of success by 50%. Again this was said very matter-of-factly. There was no way around it, we either stopped and I'd wasted this chance or we kept going.

There is no such thing as a refund for a half completed cycle, so not continuing wasn't an option.

This 50% was a huge drop in what was already a fairly low chance of success (this clinic claimed 34% success rate for a woman my age, which is considerably higher than the NHS figure). Each time, my chances of success were dropping dramatically and then I'd have to head straight back into the office. I didn't have time to absorb the information. I rarely worked from home so I got used to just shelving whatever was going on in my emotional world, the heartache from another disappointment, more bad news and just behaving as if I'd nipped out to get a sandwich or had attended a meeting in another building.

9th November 2013

I started the second lot of jabs yesterday. My tummy has a lot of needle marks and a few bruises. I was told on Friday I have a 50% reduced chance of having you now, because of some swelling in my fallopian tube, so we're now at 17% chance of this working at all. That feels really low. That's an 83% chance it won't. I have to believe it will work. IVF works for loads of couples, older than me. I know you will be in my life.

They were quite awful at the clinic. The consultant told me about the fluid, then said he'd speak to a colleague about it and he'd let me know if we should continue with this round. After a 30-minute wait, after already being an hour late for the first appointment, the nurse came to speak to me. She didn't even know about the fluid; it wasn't in my notes. She went back to speak to the consultant who had clearly forgotten all about me. She came back and asked me if I wanted to go ahead, with no further information or support making this decision. They seemed happy to continue. The consultant was supposed to be talking to his colleague, someone who knows. They are the experts. Instead the nurse comes to ask if I'm happy to continue. A nurse. They were going to let me go ahead without having surgery on my endometriosis, should I trust them? I've invested so much already; they've given me no option but to continue or to stop. To stop means to have wasted the last few months and all the money on drugs. I have to believe!

As I was just starting on my exciting adventure and creating my future, one of my best friends was nearing the end of hers. My friend from university had battled cancer for many years and had been so supportive of me doing this alone. She had been single a long time too and we found a closeness in that shared experience. We had also worked together for several years and met up regularly. We shared a lot of common experiences, and grievances with dating; with couples; with babies; with hurt. She was someone who just understood, without my needing to explain. She was selfless and uncomplaining, always positive and so incredibly brave. I saw her mid-way through my first IVF cycle. I wanted her to be a part of my baby's life, she was such an incredible influence to have in a child's life. Nine days later she died. I felt so lost.

As I progressed through the IVF cycle it became clear my eggs were not responding to the drugs, in either ovary. I was told the cycle may need to be aborted. I was heartbroken. So many hopes, such a long wait, all that money for those drugs. All the injections, the emotion, all for nothing. Another trip back into the office gutted. Somewhere I found the strength to stick on my, by now all-too familiar, office face. This was harder than I had expected. I thought making the baby would be the easy part of single motherhood. I was emotional anyway, because of the hormones and now because of the frustration that my body was letting me down.

18th November 2013

I had a scan today, my ovaries haven't responded as they should have. I have to have another scan Wednesday. Eight couples came and went today whilst I sat waiting. It made me sad, but we will have each other, and Matilda. We will be a little family. As for love, well, I'll find that too. One thing at a time.

Getting you has proven to be a huge uphill trudge, but I know I will have you, to hold in my arms and to love. It's coming up to Christmas, there is a lot of magic in the air. I know this will happen!

At the eleventh hour my right ovary picked up and in the last week of drugs it was agreed I could go ahead. Finally, I was ready for the last shot, which was the trickiest. It had to be kept in the fridge and administered exactly 10 hours before the harvesting.

Each time I left the hospital feeling exhausted, spent and alone. It was all new and overwhelming and so often difficult. Whilst waiting for the train home, I would text my friends the details of what was said or what had happened, needing a virtual hug to get me through the journey home or back to work, when I would fight tears the whole way. I am so grateful that they were always there for me, but I still felt so very alone.

As hard as I found it and with all the physical obstacles, I remained positive, I was finally becoming me, becoming who I was meant to be all along. I would be a mum. I even bought a couple of pregnancy magazines, just to read up on what it would be like, things to expect etc. Everything was focused on becoming a mum. Even things like my Boots points, I had saved almost £90 worth of points, which I just kept on saving, because I'd need all the help I could get as a single mum.

Finally, it was time for the eggs to be harvested, at which point my eggs would be mixed with the donor sperm. However, because I was using donor sperm and did not have a fresh supply, I needed to undergo ICSI (Intracytoplasmic sperm injection), which obviously cost that little bit more. This is where a sperm is injected directly into the egg, to increase chances of fertilisation. If any were successful, I would then be called in to be implanted three days later. I took the Friday off work. I knew to expect pain, this clinic did not give a choice of general anaesthetic. I was given a suppository to use one hour before the procedure. No easy task, when travelling in by public transport and knowing that no matter what time the appointment, they were always running late. Still, I made it in before I felt anything untoward occurred and waited.

I did not know what to expect. I felt like I was being swept in a tide, just doing what I was told. I was asked to get into a surgical gown and taken to the room adjacent to the embryology lab. I was given a drug, which must have been along the lines of rohypnol. The 25-30 minutes the procedure takes on average, felt like only two minutes. Everything was a blur and yet I was aware of the consultant and a nurse being there, I also remember excruciating pain when they were trying to remove the eggs from my right ovary. I remember the nurse leaning on my side with all her strength I assume to move the ovary into a better position? Then more excruciating pain, really sharp and like burning. And the pressure on my side. It felt like she was sat on me. I don't know if I screamed or if I was too drugged to, but I felt like I had, and the memory of that pain has never faded. In hindsight I suspect the dose wasn't strong enough.

I was then sent to a room to rest, with other women undergoing the same procedure. My side felt heavy with pain. The embryologist came to let me know three eggs had been harvested. I heard the lady in an adjacent bed, being told she had eight, so I knew that three was not a good number. The embryologist saw my face drop and kindly reminded me it only takes one. Tears threatened and I blinked them back. I was told to lie down until I felt a bit better and asked if someone was coming to get me? I replied no, so I was warned I should not travel home alone. I didn't know whether to scream with frustration or cry with shame. I had no choice.

Another wave of loneliness swept over me. IVF is tough, when your body seems to be an unwilling or at least, an unhelpful participant. This whole journey was surreal. And now I felt like I'd been run over. I ached. I felt dazed. I couldn't stay there forever. I told myself I had to get home, then I could relax. I dreaded it, I didn't really feel strong enough, but I wanted to get away from these people who made me feel this bad, this clinic where I felt like such a failure. I picked up my bags and slowly walked back to the station. It hurt to walk. I wanted to cry, but I didn't. I got the train and went home. I got onto my sofa with a hot water bottle, curled up into a tight ball and cried and cried. My whole insides felt agonising. That afternoon I had a temperature, which lasted all weekend. I don't actually remember moving from that curled up position on the sofa for the whole weekend, not for food, not to go to bed. Sunday afternoon I received a call from the lovely embryologist, one of my eggs could be used and I should go in the next afternoon for implantation. One egg. Weeks of hormones, invasive scans, insensitive consultants, one hugely painful procedure and I only had one egg? I couldn't believe it. More tears.

Monday morning, I got up and went into work as if nothing had happened, having previously mastered the art of slapping on a smile and styling out heartbreak, it was something I was now very accustomed to. I still didn't feel great, and was still very sore from Friday, but today was an amazing day! It's odd to know that you are doing something so incredible as creating a life whilst acting as if nothing at all were happening. At lunchtime, I travelled to the clinic. This was it; I was going to get my baby. It was going to work I knew it. I'd been through too much for it not to.

I was brought to the same room as I had been when the eggs were harvested only three days ago. It felt like a long time ago. I was asked to identify myself and confirm via the camera that the embryo was mine. When I say confirm – it was a magnified ball of cells, to identify it as mine just from how it looked would have been pretty weird. However, I could see my name was on the petri dish. The little embryo was brought into the room I was in, put under a camera, so I could watch it be sucked up into a syringe and then watch on a screen as it was implanted. I felt so emotional, seeing a tiny white blob that was my baby and seeing it again in its rightful home, in my uterus. I felt at last that my purpose in life was being achieved. I was carrying my baby. I felt like a whole person. I wanted to not move a muscle, to stay lying down and give it the best chance of staying put. I was told that I could do pretty much anything, other than swimming for three days. However, this didn't feel true. Standing up felt wrong, surely gravity would risk me losing my baby? I was terrified it would just drop out. I really wanted to stay lying down.

I got on the train; I'd never realised how much they shook. I was worried the movement might shake my baby free. I debated the merits of standing up and moving with the train or sitting but being jigged up and down and sideways. I sat, because I still felt a bit weak from the procedure on Friday. I tried to keep myself as still as possible. I went back to work that afternoon and felt like everyone would notice I was different. I felt I was glowing with pride and happiness.

30th November 2013

Little Egg was implanted. Another fun procedure, but not nearly as bad as the harvesting. It felt amazing to see you where you belong, I just wanted to stay so still and keep you safe. I have been thinking so positively, imagining Little Egg nestled into my uterus lining, like a cat in a big pillow. I've felt a lot of twinges. I really want Little Egg to be you.

I'm putting my faith in nature, that life wants to happen, this is what my body was geared to do biologically. Oh, and a sprinkling of Christmas magic!

I have a song that keeps going round in my head, Christina Perry, 'A Thousand Years', I keep singing it to

Little Egg, to you. I mean it. I have waited for you my whole life; I have loved you for such a long time. It's like all the planets are finally aligned.

The clinic had given me some progesterone to insert twice daily and gave me a guidance sheet to take home, the date for the pregnancy test was three weeks away, which at the time I didn't think about even though the consultant had said to take the test after two weeks. The whole process was such a whirlwind. It was so difficult to act like normal (whatever normal may be), whilst every part of my being felt like it was different. After a few days I felt a strong twinge, so sharp I almost fell over, but it was a split second. After that, I felt more twinges every now and then. I spoke to a friend who said this was a very good sign, that it was Little Egg attaching.

Every evening I would talk to Little Egg. I'd imagine that my uterus lining was like a deep, soft cushion that Little Egg would bury into and be safe and protected. I was sure Little Egg was attached; I could feel him. My uterus felt alive, I felt amazing. My whole raison d'etre finally happening. I started thinking about when the baby would be due, and more importantly, when I could start maternity leave and have a break from mundane work. My baby would be born in August 2014. My true life would begin in August 2014.

9th December 2013

Yesterday I had bad cramps, I couldn't concentrate on work. I was so worried I was losing Little Egg; I so want it to be you! Celebrating Christmas with you is what I've always wanted, why I've put myself through all this. I hope you can understand why I've done this. There may be a time when you wish I'd not made this choice, but there will never be a time when I do. I love you so much already, I just need you here to show you.

I've been listening to a beautiful piece of music and I think of you, I think of rocking you to sleep with it playing, it's called Seal Lullaby. I wonder if you can hear it? I read that you can recognise music you heard in the womb once you are born.

I am so looking forward to meeting you and starting our amazing adventure together. I know we will be happy.

Later that day, I started feeling very painful cramps and then bleeding, very lightly, this did not feel right, but I did some research online and it seemed spotting was common in early pregnancy, particularly following IVF. I tried to stay calm.

10th December 2013

I've had some cramps and had some blood. I am so scared I'm losing Little Egg! I'm trying so hard to stay positive, but it's hard, this doesn't feel right, I don't feel right. I'm feeling very lonely and angry, that I have to work so hard for this, when I should have a man who loves me and sperm on tap. It shouldn't be this difficult just to have a baby.

I've had a look and apparently some women have cramping and spotting during implantation. Some people also continue having periods. I so want you to be ok. I can't lose you. I've only ever wanted to be a mum. Hang on Little Egg.

The following day, I was in a great deal of pain all day at work, I knew things were not right. I remember the Wednesday evening, being on the point of passing out in pain, stood on a very busy commuter train on my way home, I couldn't move left or right because of the crowd. It felt stiflingly hot as I held onto my stomach to try to contain the pain and opening a window to just have a little fresh air to breathe. A woman who was sat down near the window had such a go at me about it. I was in such agony, I couldn't really hear her, I just hoped that I would make it at least to the next stop before passing out. I could barely stand and knew I was losing my baby, I felt completely separated from the world around me, similar to when I'd gone over in my car. Time felt different.

I made it home from the station very slowly and then rushed straight to the toilet. I knew it was over. I have never seen so much blood and it felt very surreal to see it all coming out of me at such a fast flow. I wondered briefly how much I could lose before it became dangerous. I considered calling an ambulance but did not have the energy to get up and find my phone. It just kept coming. At one point there was a tiny, smooth blood clot. I wondered if that was the egg sac? Would it have been that big so early on? I would only have been five weeks pregnant. I suspect not, but I'll never know. However, seeing that stayed with me.

I finally made it to my bed and did not move except when absolutely necessary. My beautiful little cat stayed with me the whole time. I had my phone dialled on 999 that first night because I felt so weak and was in so much pain, I genuinely didn't think I would make it. I had called 111 earlier as I worried it may have been a ruptured ectopic pregnancy but was told I could wait until morning. Thankfully, since I didn't feel up to moving. I was curled up in a tight ball. The waves of pain were so excruciating that I felt I might pass out, I may have done, the whole night is a blur.

I text my boss in the morning and told her I had suspected appendicitis, since some of my team had seen me doubled in pain as I left, I thought this sounded feasible. I took the following few days off. I called the clinic the next day and the nurse I spoke to said the round had simply failed. I insisted I was having a miscarriage, but the handwritten note I had said I was due to take the test the following day. I later learnt that this had been a mistake and it should have been the week before, after two weeks, which is what the consultant had originally said and which would have saved a lot of heartache in how I was treated.

The nurse insisted this was definitely just a failed round and this was just a heavy period. I've had periods since I was 12. Every month. This was not a period. When I was able to, spurred on by my desire to prove the existence of my baby, I walked to the little shop close by to buy a pregnancy test. I took it and it came back positive. I would not have my baby dismissed so casually. I called again to tell her this and insisted they see me. She begrudgingly set up an appointment for the following day.

At the clinic I saw the same nurse I had spoken to and she again treated me like a neurotic woman who was just wishful thinking. However, to appease me she took a blood test and requested a urine sample. When she returned with the results, she confirmed I had been pregnant but with my symptoms, there was no longer a pregnancy. No hint of apology or any sympathy. This woman has clearly never suffered a miscarriage. She was so unbelievably dismissive not only of the emotional pain but the physical pain. In dismissing my pregnancy, it made me feel like my sense of loss wasn't valid. Little Egg was gone, and no one knew he'd been there, that he'd existed. I was sent on my way and told I would have an appointment made with a consultant for the New Year.

There it was, on the 11th December 2013 I lost my first baby. Just a short month after losing my wonderful friend. I was heartbroken and felt entirely alone. But, I had been pregnant. I had been a mum for the briefest of times. In pregnancy terms I'd have been just five weeks. A very early loss, but such a long journey to have got there. My dream however, felt almost more within my grasp. The next time would work. I had been pregnant. I had felt pregnant. I was heartbroken but felt alive. I was even more sure that motherhood was not just an expectation but an absolute core part of who I am. I had felt absolutely amazing being pregnant. I was sure my body would know what to do next time, this was just a trial run. Quite a few women lose their first pregnancy, almost like the body is just warming up.

The pain and bleeding continued for the following few days. The bleeding had subsided to that of a normal period. The pain would come on in waves of cramps. Nothing prepared me for the severity of the miscarriage cramps. That weekend I had a group of friends coming round for a Christmas gathering, so

Saturday morning I went food shopping. Unfortunately, one of these waves came on just as I was heading back to my car with my shopping. My legs gave way with the intensity and I collapsed into a crouched position.

A kind lady stopped and asked if I was ok? I replied that I would be fine, inside my head I screamed at her, “I’ve lost my baby!” She asked if I had someone I could call, I said yes, to save face. I went and sat in my car hoping the wave would pass, it was not. I wondered again whether to call an ambulance, but I didn’t want to leave my cat alone, besides, all I wanted was to be home and get into bed and disappear under the duvet. I drove home, slowly, with both front windows wound right down, chatting to myself the whole time to make sure I stayed conscious.

My friends came round the following day to celebrate Christmas, with their young children. At the time it hurt, but in hindsight now I see how much worse it would get. I think emotional pain is balanced by hope. The more hope you have, the less severe the emotional pain. Circumstances change the experience of a miscarriage. I had waited years to become a mum and was so incredibly sad and disappointed. I had been through a lot to get there, but I could afford another round of IVF, so the hope was still there. My mum had a miscarriage, they happen. I was still on the right road and getting closer to the destination. I felt that my body knew what it was doing now, next time would definitely work. I was full of hope.

I had been working out of a different office that fateful Wednesday, and I was able to work from home the following week and then I was off for two weeks anyway over Christmas, therefore avoiding any questions or conversations. When I did go back in, the guy on my team said, "you must have had what I had just before Christmas", I went with it, what was I going to say? I had not booked flights to see my family at Christmas, since I am terrified of flying and felt that such high levels of adrenalin would not be good in the first few weeks of pregnancy.

Once I lost the baby, my family asked me to come over, but I just wanted to sit quietly. I didn't want to make conversation or be ok or experience the most family orientated day of my year, having just lost my little family. So, I spent my first ever Christmas alone. I had several invitations to go and join friends and their families, which I really appreciated, but I could not face the banality of socialising or polite chitchat.

The end of this year had been tough, I lost an amazing friend and lost my tiny baby. I wanted a New Year to start, to just leave this one behind. 2014 had a lucky ring to it, this would be my year, everything would change, my life would start this year.

My little life

You were there, now you are not
I was a mum, with no child
But I had you, for the shortest time
At last I felt complete
My missing limb returned
You were not to be
The cruelty that it was my little life
taken, no one else's
Unfair

It felt so right to have you
Why did you have to go?
I loved you so much already
The pain of losing you in body and spirit
Like nothing else in the world
And now I have nothing to show
For the weeks that we were together
Seems to all the world that you weren't
really there
But I know

I wish I could turn back time
Its lonely without you
So many important dates now mean
nothing
Who am I now?

Life is empty even though you never were
You, my missing limb
So small and yet so mighty
My love
My little life

January 2014

Paulo

I counted down impatiently for the next visit to the clinic. I wanted to get straight back on it. The nurse had felt that I needed time to get over the miscarriage. The miscarriage she hadn't wanted to believe in. I read up online that some consultants recommended waiting at least six months, others just one month. I had waited too long already. I kept calling to see if there was a cancellation I could take. Nothing was going to stop me this time, by next Christmas I would be a mum.

This may sound odd, considering where I was in my journey to single motherhood, but I had not given up on finding love. I had separated the two in my mind. I did not want to be with someone just to create a family, I wanted to be with them because of who they were, who we were as a couple. I also had to be a mum and could not stop now, about to become 38 years old, I had waited too long already. I recently joined a new dating website, with the encouragement of a friend, who called it 'operation Lone Wolf'. He was determined I'd find someone. This, I felt, was my last attempt. Over the Christmas holidays I had started talking to a very nice guy. We quickly moved from messaging via the website to texting and soon we were texting several times every day. He made me laugh and seemed very genuine. After a month of talking I asked him whether we were just going to just be pen pals? He got the hint and asked me out on a date. I really enjoyed his company and we proceeded to have a date every week after that.

When my appointment finally came around, the consultant showed far more sympathy than the nurse had. He said that it was good news I had been able to get pregnant. I had to have another scan. It turned out I still had fluid in one of my tubes. This could well be why I miscarried, if this fluid had got into my uterus. They needed to investigate since I may need it to be cut out or I'd never be able to carry a child to term. BUT....it was the right tube, on the side of my only working ovary, therefore I would never be able to fall pregnant naturally, only IVF could ever work and the odds of that, very slim. Wow! Cut out my fallopian tube, casually thrown into the conversation, as if this was some innocuous growth, not a vital part of my reproductive system. Bad news again. Floored again. I left the clinic feeling heavy, with my dreams shattered.

The consultant had thought the fluid in the tube may have dated back to my surgery. At the time, I suspected it was more likely to be from the harvesting of my eggs which had been so painful, with the nurse leaning on my side. I had a temperature after it, which would indicate an infection, certainly a massive reaction to the procedure by my immune system. I had suspected this wasn't right at the time. I didn't much like the way I'd been treated by this clinic from the start. I doubted their care for me and investment in a positive outcome because they had been willing to go ahead without treating the endometriosis, but after the harvesting, I felt I couldn't trust them either. It had felt shambolic, amateurish and frightening. However, they had told me there was liquid in one of my tubes ahead of the harvesting. They hadn't really been very helpful at the time, so maybe it was because of the surgery.

In hindsight, I should have asked for my embryo to be frozen, until the liquid in the tube was gone, but this wasn't offered as a choice, it was continue or not. I trusted these doctors to know what to do. I'd paid so much; I couldn't afford to just scrap that round. In hindsight also, I should have moved clinic now, but I felt a bit stuck. I'd have had to start again from scratch, blood tests, new sperm donor. I liked this donor and this would slow me down. I didn't really know what to do about it. I cried all day after the news. Back to work the next day with my fixed 'I'm fine' face, but I couldn't really concentrate much. I was so angry that this had happened. It was their responsibility to guide me as to the best outcome, they had just gone ahead with this liquid which, it seemed clear to me, had caused the miscarriage. I felt sure that if the procedure hadn't been so disastrous, then there would have been no liquid and my baby would have lived.

IVF is daunting, you are already in a fragile position since for whatever reason, this is your means to have a family. I had regularly received bad news during appointments at this clinic which were never done with kindness or support. The experience of the harvesting had left me feeling quite vulnerable. I had been aware of being in such a lot of pain but unable to express this and at no point was this recognised by the clinic. Since I was conscious throughout, they must have seen I was in pain? I had just trusted these doctors. I had been referred to this clinic, in hindsight maybe I should have been more involved in this, done some research on various clinics and asked to be referred to a specific one. Since I ended up paying anyway, there must have been countless clinics to chose from.

Considering how much research I usually do, the fact I didn't look into this more surprises me now. I think emotionally I was in a difficult place, heartbroken that I was having to do this alone, but also expecting that one fertility clinic would be like any other fertility clinic. I'm not sure if there were reviews available. I should have looked.

I think women need more support starting this kind of journey. More information about what to expect, not just statistics about chances of success and what they can do with any left over embryos. When I did my first round of IVF, I did not know of anyone else who had been through it to speak to. It just wasn't talked about, as if it were somehow shameful. Perhaps why I'd not looked for reviews? The fact remains that empathy seemed to be lacking in this particular clinic.

When I started my counselling training I remember a doctor being in the class. He felt that his training had lacked the human element of dealing with patients and felt an understanding of the basics of counselling would provide that. I hadn't put the two together at the time, but this missing element in the training was very evident in this particular clinic. I am also aware that now there is a lot of support online, the Trying to Conceive (TTC) community is growing. I was however not aware of this when I started this journey. I suspect it has grown hugely over the last few years so may not have been present at all in 2014.

30th January 2014

I've called every week since Christmas, to see if an earlier appointment had become available, nothing doing. So, the day finally arrived. We talked about why I lost Little Egg. The consultant said if it was due to the endometriosis, then it would likely happen again, although he did say it was unlikely so soon after it was operated on. Phew.

He also mentioned the liquid in my fallopian tube. I can't believe it could have been that? Why didn't they freeze my egg and wait for my infection to go? They knew about the liquid. Why didn't I know to ask? Maybe I should have researched more? But you feel compelled to answer immediately, I was taking the drugs. I feel so betrayed by the clinic. They are the experts. I feel so naïve in this journey, just pressing ahead with the scant information they give me.

More waiting, more tests at various times of my cycle. However, the following tests showed the liquid level had dropped. This made me think it can't have been due to the surgery last June, if it could reduce that quickly? Maybe it was made worse by my infection after the harvesting? Still, what a relief. If I was going to have another try, it needed to be soon. My egg quantity was very low, so the consultant said we need to start as soon as possible. They're giving me one more round using my eggs and if they don't respond then I'll need donor eggs. He said, so matter-of-factly.

Clearly this guy had overslept the day of the bedside manner lecture at University. He didn't seem to register that this was crushing news. Yet again. My dreams, my genes just casually thrown away. He didn't seem to know or care why I was doing IVF, why I wanted to have my own genes, linked to the people I'd lost, or was losing, to keep that ongoing connection. To have a child which was mine, entirely. We never spoke about who I was and what had led me to this, it was purely transactional. He didn't seem to realise that I was having to pay for this alone, that it was excruciatingly expensive, I wasn't able to have endless rounds of IVF. This round HAD to work.

I left the clinic once more with crushing news to digest. I was so completely gutted. Donor eggs. So, my child won't have any traits from my mum or my dad or grandma, both of which I'd lost years before. Or, of me. No genetic link. And that's just if it works, but odds of IVF are pretty small at my age. You notice the odds when you are paying for them. It was huge news to absorb and yet I just wanted to plough ahead, whatever it took to have a baby, to be a mum, to feel whole. Once again, I got home and cried. Not my baby, not my genes. I felt a huge weight of loss. However, my need for motherhood was greater, no time to stop and think about it, I had to just keep going, keep trying.

At this stage I didn't even stop to think about all the other repercussions of using donor eggs, the fact that there would be another biological mother. The more complex life story this would lead to for my child. I had worried about how to explain a sperm donor and single motherhood, but now I'd be carrying a child which was neither genetically mine, nor my partners. What would that feel like for my child? What would that feel like for me? I think I was so optimistic that this would happen this time that I didn't really think of it as a real option.

This round would work, I was sure. We had got so close with the first round.

We were starting another round and that had to be hopeful. We agreed that I should try a different drug mix, which may help the eggs respond quicker and he gave me a prescription for the required drugs. These were even more expensive, almost £2,000 for only a few weeks of drugs. I called Lewisham Council to see if their policy had changed. No, I was still single, therefore still all on me. My fault for not finding a man, (or woman) with which to share my life. My life-long horror and disappointment in the pharmaceutical world was reinforced by the cost of these mass-produced drugs. I had no choice, I needed the drugs, so I paid out. This time, to not arouse suspicion, I had these delivered to my home address. Luckily, I didn't have to undergo the mini menopause this time, I went straight from the pill to overstimulation of ovaries.

I found out that a colleague at work had been through IVF and asked her if we could talk about it? I needed to speak to someone who understood, the first round had been too lonely. We went to get a coffee outside of the office. There were some roadworks happening on the pavement opposite as we walked along. I noticed a pram with a very small boy coming in the opposite direction. He was facing forwards and as his dad pushed him past the roadworks, the terrified little boy was screaming out. My whole body felt like it was being pulled towards him, my uterus cramped up,

I wanted to hold him and comfort him. It felt like a force stronger than gravity pulling me towards him.

Due to the noise of the drilling, his father did not notice until he'd walked past the roadworks, by which time I already had tears rolling down my face with the need to comfort this beautiful little baby boy in his terror. I had been quite shocked by the ferocity of my physical pull towards this baby in distress. The colleague I was with noticed me looking over and acknowledged that she too would notice every baby when she had been desperately trying to conceive. Luckily, I don't think she'd noticed the tears, we were walking side by side, so I'd obviously managed to remove the evidence unnoticed and I'd pulled myself together by the time we got to the coffee shop.

I was surprised that what had felt like such a strong physical pull had appeared to the outside world like a casual glance over to a baby. It was surreal, like those time travel films, when the heroes have been gone seconds but they have actually experienced years. When it's all you want, but seems so out of reach, it seems the world is flooded with beautiful babies, surrounding you, but none of them is yours to love.

I began the IVF drugs on my next period. I had only just met this new man and did not feel this was the right time to let him know I was undergoing IVF. However, following my disappointment at having wasted six months with the last relationship the previous year, I was not willing to waste more of my precious fertile years on the off chance something may come of this. I reminded myself love has no age limit, but fertility does. I talked it over with my friends, when should I tell him? What if I had a miscarriage again, then there would be no reason to put such a new and exciting relationship under such strain for nothing. I did not yet know when I would tell him, but I knew it was not yet. I loved getting to know this guy, I didn't want to lose him, and I was sure I would.

He would mostly stay round mine, since I lived alone and had a cat to look after, whereas he shared a flat. I would sneak off at the same time in the evening to go and inject the drugs, the whole time worrying about what he was thinking, what was I doing for 20 minutes at 11pm every night and what I would say if he asked? He didn't and when we later talked about it, he hadn't even realised I would disappear for that long.

I was back to having regular internal scans. Always with a male consultant too. I'm not prudish, but come on, every other week during an IVF cycle? My ovary was struggling again, so it was touch and go whether this cycle would need to be stopped again. Another reason I waited to tell my new boyfriend (there, I said it). Why risk breaking something good if it's not even going to happen? I didn't like the deception though and felt a lot of guilt about it. I'm not good at secrets and I don't like them, so the fact I held on as long as I did is a testament to how driven I was to become a mum. It was difficult getting more bad news at every scan and then having to be an engaging and smiley date, when I just wanted to cry.

I was due to have my eggs harvested the next week and that weekend together had been so lovely. I knew I had to tell him now. This weekend had marked a shift from just dating. He was my boyfriend. It was not fair to keep seeing him with the possibility I could end up carrying someone else's child. I delayed because I felt sure that he would run for the hills. Of course, he would. What a crazy thing to be doing by yourself, he'd not get it. He'd not want to be part of this crazy plan. I felt sure he'd leave. I was wrong. He was shocked at the news and found it difficult, but he stayed.

After the trauma of last time, a friend was coming with me and would take me home after the harvesting. My ovary again had been very slow to respond, but again, at the 11th hour had kicked into action and in the end, I got five eggs. This time I had a senior consultant carry out the harvesting and I barely felt a thing. There was no one leaning on my side, no excruciating pain and no fever afterwards, it was almost a walk in the park. This only served to reinforce my view that what happened last time was down to negligence and I suspect why I miscarried my first baby. I'm not sure why I didn't say or do anything. I think I found the whole experience of IVF by myself quite overwhelming and didn't really know which way was up, during that first round. Thinking about it, I lost a close friend, just as I was doing my cycle, so still in shock from that, as well as going through quite a frightening process by myself.

A part of me also couldn't believe this is where my life was. That I was needing to do this when others just find love and make babies the traditional way. When I think back to that period, I feel like I was a rabbit in headlights, tumbling along whichever direction I was sent, with no real sense of control.

I got the call, three eggs had fertilised, I was due to be implanted the next day. My boyfriend, Paulo told me that he found it really difficult, but that he wished me well for the day, such a surreal conversation. I was upset we'd not met years ago. Why hadn't he looked for me sooner? I had been looking for him! Once I got to the clinic, I was told that only two eggs had continued to develop in the required way overnight, bit of a blow. But these were two very good eggs, in the top category. I was sure this was it; this was my time. Again, I saw my perfect two eggs implanted and felt that warm glow of knowing you are carrying a baby. I willed them to attach and stay.

13th March 2014

I had 2 little eggs put in today. Timing could not be worse; I've met such a lovely man. I would love him to be your dad. But I cannot hold off, what if it doesn't work between us? I don't want to have to make a choice between motherhood or love, they should both come together, that's what happens normally. I'm sorry I'm doing this all backwards for you.

I know that one of these little eggs is you. They were top category, because of how they'd be splitting since they were fertilised. This time my body will know what its doing. This time its you. I daren't hope that you might actually have a dad too, its too soon, but I'll try my best.

I was so positive this time, that I didn't talk to the eggs. I also didn't really do the positive visualisations of comfy cushions. I was enjoying myself with Paulo. Turned out he loved gardening also and was helping me put my stamp on the bungalow garden. He was now generally round every Friday night through to Monday morning and we'd usually have a date on Wednesday night also. I merrily allowed Little Eggs two and three to work their magic and waited the required two weeks to take my obviously positive test.

22nd March 2014

I've not had any twinges this time. I don't feel different. I'm trying hard not to worry. After all Little Egg didn't do too well in the end, so feeling different is probably a good thing. Today I even felt like my period was about to start, it hasn't yet - good sign!

Two weeks later, instead of that positive test, I had a period. I was shocked! I had been so sure. I didn't even lose these perfect little eggs, they never attached to start with. I was incredibly disappointed, I felt like I'd failed somehow. Was it because I hadn't visualised? Or not talked to the little eggs? I hadn't thought about them enough. I was worried I had been paying too much attention to my boyfriend and life other than motherhood. I would remind myself that some people go a few months without knowing they are pregnant, the eggs would have been none the wiser as to what I was thinking about. But, I also thought about the fact life wants to happen. I had two highest category eggs and neither had attached. Little Egg in November last year was not as good a quality, he'd attached just fine. Why had these not? A drug addict, living on the streets, eating crap food if at all, can get pregnant by mistake and carry to term and yet I had actively put the two perfect eggs in my uterus, I had been so careful, I had been eating really healthily, and nothing.

4th April 2014

Last Monday my period started. It hurt too much to write at the time. I ache for my children, I have so much love for them, but they're not here.

You're not here. Everything I do is to make life good for you, to build our life together. I'm devastated and so scared I won't have my own babies. I don't know how to feel better? I think I need time away from IVF, pumping all these hormones cannot be healthy.

I grieved after that cycle, even with no actual pregnancy, no baby had been lost. I grieved for the opportunity, for the two little eggs which could have been my child. I grieved for my motherhood. I had been so sure. At the same time, I now had hope that I could potentially have something real with Paulo and we could make our own babies. Maybe this was the way it was supposed to be?

I was on this life high of being able to make babies the old-fashioned way now, when I went in for my next appointment with the consultant in early May. The consultant explained that my ovaries did not respond well enough to the drugs and that I have a low reserve, meaning I have very few eggs left now. Since the endometriosis had destroyed one of my ovaries, I was down half on the meagre amount. He said that the chances of me ever carrying my own child were remote. I felt like I'd been punched. What did he just say? I looked at the consultant who didn't seem to realise he'd floored me with his punch. He carried on talking about something. I remember realising his room was quite small with no window. I needed a window. I needed to get out of this room.

What is it with this clinic and unbearably bad news? This time I barely bothered stopping the tears on the journey home. I cried, only hanging on until I was home for the full-blown loud, undignified sobs. Everything my life was about, everything I thought I would be, reduced to a half hour conversation with a consultant letting me know it was unlikely and then releasing me back into civilisation. The unfairness of it overwhelmed me. How? How can the very biological essence of being female not happen for me? How could something I have so desperately wanted, for such a long time, be taken away? I had done everything in my power to avoid this very scenario.

I always believed that there was no such thing as luck or fate, that you make your own destiny by the choices you make and the proactiveness of your behaviour. I had done everything I could. I was inconsolable and it took everything to get up in the morning and not cry continuously during the next few days. I wasn't ill so felt guilty taking time off work, just because my whole world had collapsed around me. I felt such rage against nature, the world, the galaxy, against mothers I would see in the street, not behaving how I felt they should. I was furious that there were young teenagers falling pregnant at the drop of a hat, why had I been so careful not to, when I was young? Had I known what I knew now.

I started seeing my miscarriage the year before differently, that had been my child. I had that child, he was there and was snatched away. That was my last opportunity and because of what I felt was very poor medical care by the clinic, I had lost him. It was no longer a positive first step. It was my only step, my last step to motherhood. The pain of that first loss increased as the significance of it was revealed. That was my only baby.

I was so hurt seeing families, mothers, babies, seemingly everywhere. I felt betrayed by nature when people just got pregnant and carried to term, without even really thinking about it. Tears were never far from the surface. I could not cope with the amount of 'happy' announcements on Facebook, nor the constant barrage of family photographs and gushing of mother's love for their children, everything I couldn't have. Also posts of annoyance of their children, doing this, not doing that. Did they not realise the gift they had? I felt so outside of life, alone. I stopped looking altogether.

The rage didn't stop there, women, with zero bump yet, but already proudly sporting one of the 'baby on board' badges were also subject to my rage, with their smug little badges. Whoopie for you and your fertile loins. Not that they knew. Like a swan gliding peacefully across a still lake, whilst if you look underneath the water, the legs are paddling like crazy. I had a calm, 'normal' exterior whilst inside my head, the emotions jostled for prime position, sorrow, fear, hopelessness and rage. I rarely let my rage out.

Hopelessness was most often the winner. Every time I put the television on, there were families, babies, happiness, nappy adverts, baby milk adverts, pregnancy test adverts. Colleagues at work were having babies. I felt like the odd one out, like something must be wrong. Maybe life had simply forgotten I was here and that I too, should be part of the circle of life?

One of my close friends got pregnant with her third child, unintentionally. She sent me the most beautiful note telling me that she knew the news would hurt. I felt so awful, how could I resent someone else having a baby? But it did hurt. I had just been told I was unlikely to be able to have my own at all. It felt like it should have been my turn. I weirdly felt that a pregnancy elsewhere would somehow reduce my chances further. As if there are some universal scales, where if one person was having a baby, it means another cannot. I know, it sounds ridiculous. A broken heart doesn't necessarily have much logic to its thoughts, it just hurts and tries to make sense of what it's going through.

I was becoming more withdrawn. I didn't want to talk or see people who were pregnant or had a young family. Finally I accepted that this wasn't a nightmare I'd wake up from, it was not going away, people were going to continue having babies and discussing their families, life goes on and I was the one who was different. I was the one who was outside the norm. I was the one who had to learn how to deal with all my emotions and my loss.

I decided perhaps counselling would help. I could get this through work, so I called the number from one of the meeting rooms, where I ended up sobbing through my story about not being able to have a child of my own, after having lost my one chance, possibly through the fault of the clinic. I was shocked at how close to the surface my despair was. I was in work, in a meeting room with glass walls. I mean, I don't show emotion. I talk about it, yes. I can talk about it all day long. I can tell you how I feel, almost as if I'm talking about someone else, but I won't show it. I said I wanted a female counsellor, since I suspected a man would not be able to understand how it feels for the very meaning of my womanhood to be called into question, or for your uterus to do back flips when it hears a baby cry. I was called back the next day, by a gentleman. I told him that I had specifically asked for a female counsellor. He got defensive and told me he was trained and would be able to work with me regardless of my issue. I wasn't ready to try and explain my pain, I was only just learning about it myself. I wanted someone who would just understand it.

I was able to find a female counsellor locally but was dreading going. To me, it signified a lack of strength and resilience which I was not happy to admit. The first session was amazing. I sat down and told the counsellor what had happened over the last few months and that I'd been told I was unlikely to ever carry my own child. The counsellor told me that my feelings of anger and sadness were perfectly justified. I was grieving for something I had lost, not just my longed for and loved baby, but also an opportunity, the chance of ever carrying my own child to term. I had lost a piece of my life story.

I felt a huge wave of relief, as her words clicked into place. I wasn't just a mean, jealous lady who couldn't manage life. I was grieving. At last I felt validated in the overwhelming sadness that had been consuming me for weeks and I sobbed for the remainder of the session. I had really needed that release. That acknowledgement that I wasn't weak, I had a genuine reason to feel this awful. The following week the session was completely different. I was so positive. I was told the chance of carrying my own child was remote, not that it definitely could not happen. That was the glimmer of hope I needed. I just needed to bring this into what was still a fairly new relationship. This would work. My ability to find hope is nothing if not resilient. It just keeps bouncing back.

The counsellor gave me a list of three websites linked to infertility. Since I had been feeling alone on a barren island (pun absolutely intended), I was almost relieved that there were websites. However, I was not prepared for what I found. The first site I looked at had an article written by a lady now in her 60's, regarding her journey to accepting her childlessness. As I read the article, about her finding other things in life, which bought fulfilment, like travelling, I felt my hope being sucked out of me like I had a resident dementor. How can you just give up? Accept this is how it is? I found myself also thinking she obviously did not need children, because not having them is simply not an option for me. Now I regret my cruel judgement of a woman who had faced devastating childlessness and conquered to find meaning in her life, but at the time I couldn't see it, I didn't want to accept a life without children, I didn't want this to be my life. I didn't want to be put in the same boat as this woman.

Even if I end up not being able to have my own, I will have a family, I would adopt. I didn't even look at the other sites, I gave them up as a bad job. I did not want to read more depressing stories, I was looking for hope, for kindred spirits who fought and conquered. At the time I felt the only way of conquering infertility was by having a baby. I was angry too with my counsellor, did she think it wouldn't happen? Was she looking for acceptance from me? Did she want me to make my peace with the news I couldn't carry my own child and just move on, as if it was just a product that had sold out? This was my life, the very essence of who I was. I was absolutely not taking no for an answer!

I read an article in the paper at around the same time, a woman, again in her 60's, talking about her experience of the heartache of watching her friends one by one have the babies she too longed for, the pain of which had diminished as they had grown up but, it was accentuated again now that her friends were becoming grandmothers, another joy denied to her. Reading this filled me with a sense of dread. I have to avoid this, at all costs. I cannot face heartache at every turn. I need a family of my own. I cannot, will not, ever use the phrase "I couldn't have children". I can't accept this would be my life. I was meant to be a mum; I am a mum. I just haven't got my babies yet.

15th August 2014

My darling Little Egg, you'd have been born this week. If you knew how my heart breaks. I have been so sad, so heartbroken, so angry. What I hate most is my complete lack of power over this. I can't do a thing. I loved you for the shortest period of life that I had you.

I read a little poem that I love, it said, "I carried you for every second of your life and I will love you for every second of mine". It made me cry. I did love you. I loved who you would become, I loved who I was going to be with you. I think I'll come into my own being a mum, it's a role I'm supposed to play. I wish you were here. I had so much love for you. I do still love the thought of you. The you, you would have been. The me you'd have made me be.

I'm so sad I lost you, especially if you were my only chance at a child of my own. I want to believe this isn't true, not because I would love my baby any less from a donor egg, but because I so *hoped to see parts of my family and of me in you.*

Paulo was far more relaxed about my news about ever carrying a baby of my own and didn't seem feel the same sense of 'now or never'. He also felt a little pressured by me, completely fair enough really. I didn't want him to think that I was only with him to make babies, because this was truly not the case. I had not been alone for such a long time, avoiding settling for just anyone, to then succumb in the end. I was with him for him. We had an amazing connection. I had fallen completely in love with him and believed he was Soulmate #2. I didn't want to lose him over this, now I had found him, but I also did not want to waste more precious fertile months. I needed him to understand that if he wanted children and if he wanted them with me, then it was now. He'd not really thought about it yet, I tried so hard not to push the issue, but I was 38, there is no escaping the fact my time was running out fast and I felt its pressure as a physical burden on me.

We're pregnant!

The hurt of not being a mum never ceased. It felt like a missing limb. The feelings I had of a physical ache within my body for a baby just strengthened. The families around me continued to be a bittersweet experience of love for friends and the weird sense of being in a parallel world. With all my chasing of motherhood, it sometimes felt that motherhood was actually chasing me, it was there at every turn, making its presence known, making my lack of it felt deeply. With friends, at work, on the telly, everywhere motherhood. The good, the bad, the ugly of it, but all of it, was something I felt made me incomplete.

After some gentle persuasion, we started trying that autumn, I so hoped to be pregnant before Christmas, although realistically didn't expect it. For some reason that's the marker. That's when my lack of motherhood hurts the most. That is when I have the best memories from my childhood. I also think its linked to the end of a year, having achieved something, having moved on from the nobody drifting through life unnoticed. The weight of the previous year can be heavy if you don't feel you've achieved what you should have. If I was pregnant, I'd have conquered.

Over the last couple of years, periods had become such a feature in my life, they were a constant reminder of a lost opportunity. Of time moving on. Appointments were dictated by them, drugs were coordinated with them, scans worked around them. When you want to be pregnant, their appearance is always accompanied by a crushing heartache, signifying what hadn't happened yet again. I think those who go through any kind of infertility or difficulty staying pregnant for whatever reason, have such a painful relationship with their body. You feel so betrayed.

14th November 2014

I have struggled at college, every week I'm being told about the joys of parenthood. Childlessness feels like an invisible disability, it's a constant ache. It affects my every waking hour and my whole future. No one would dream of talking to someone in a wheelchair about the virtues of legs, of how amazing it is to have them and what it feels like to run with them. Or even mention the annoyances of walking, for example stubbing a toe. Yet I am constantly subjected to the amazing virtues of motherhood as well as its pitfalls, because that's the norm, people have children, that's just what happens. Each sentence to me feels like a knife in my heart. Something else I can't feel for my child. Another reason I don't fit in.

People have regularly dropped into conversation, that I cannot begin to understand the bond between a mother and a child, not having a child of my own. Firstly, the hurt caused by that comment is excruciating. But also, I have never heard such insulting rubbish. The smugness of it. I had an amazing bond with my mum, I know what a bond between mother and child can be. If I didn't know, would I have fought so hard just to feel it? The only thing not being understood is my all-consuming anguish of not being able to feel the bond from the mother's side, for myself. Women take it for granted. I am overwhelmed by maternal feelings and the urgency to hold a child of my own.

The unfairness of knowing that the consultant may have been right, I may not be able to carry a child of my own. There are so many women out there who were not bothered about having children, but have them fills me with such anger, overtaken only by my ugly jealousy of all those who have managed to carry their first pregnancy to term. What if my first pregnancy will be my only pregnancy?

At Christmas I went to be with my family in Switzerland. I assumed that it would not happen this quickly so helped myself to a few glasses of wine. I remember Christmas day feeling like I might be pregnant, I felt more alive, but then told myself that was just wishful thinking, we'd literally just been trying for three months. I always feel the magic of Christmas time, I think because it always felt so magical as a child. It's the only time my whole family are together, and I love it, but recently I'd felt excluded there too. My older cousins have children, Christmas is all about children and family. My mum would so love to be a grandmother. Now it just makes Christmas harder. I want to share that magic with my own child. I want my own family.

When I got home, again I had some champagne for New Year and then spent the remainder of my time off work clearing up the garden, raking up leaves, cleaning, tidying, all energetic, lifting, moving heavy items. All things which I worried about doing, in case it would ruin chances of pregnancy, whilst also not wanting to be unrealistic or ridiculous, not doing things which needed to be done, just in case. The day my period was due, it didn't arrive and that night I was incredibly hot.

That morning I suspected I may be pregnant, I felt different, without being able to pinpoint exactly how. I said nothing and waited for my period to start. Again, it did not and again that night I was like a furnace. The following day I took a test and it was positive. I was overjoyed! I went into the hallway and asked Paulo if he was ok about an early morning surprise? He told me to go on, so I told him the good news. He confided later that he had become very emotional on the drive into work. This was it. Our baby, our family. Now my life could really start.

9th January 2015

I can't believe it, I'm pregnant, you are here! I thought we'd probably need IVF because of my lack of eggs, the consultant had seemed so sure I'd not carry my own child, but here you are. I've had all sorts of symptoms but whenever they stop, even for a short time, I panic, that I'm having another miscarriage. I get flashbacks to being on the loo. I want to be so excited, but part of me is so scared. On the plus side, I've been pregnant longer than ever before, that has to be a good sign.

I didn't know what to do next, I wanted to shout the news from the rooftops, but its frowned upon so soon. I found an app for my phone which told you day by day what to expect, what progress your baby was making and allowed you to log your own symptoms. I was having mild cramps, nausea, migraines and was feeling ever so tired. I felt amazing. Even better when the pregnancy symptoms were at their worst. I felt alive. I loved the fact I felt sick. I loved the fact I couldn't stay awake beyond 9pm, some days even 8pm. I loved every second of being pregnant. I was holding my baby. My darling, longed for baby was here, where he belonged. Every symptom just meant my baby was here, at last.

I called the doctor and was told by a receptionist that they didn't deal with pregnancies and I would need to find a local midwife and was given a number. The number went to voicemail but also said I could book online, so I went onto the local Health authority website and found the correct form. I submitted this and waited. After two weeks I had heard nothing, so I contacted them again, again nothing. In the end I called and explained I had submitted a form three weeks ago and another one week ago, the person I spoke to said I would hear back shortly. Half an hour later I received a text message with my booking appointment confirmation – two more weeks to wait.

Every day I would count down the days for the following week. I would check how big my baby was, how much more development had happened, which parts of the baby were now forming. Every day, I felt more confident, every day I was pregnant meant that much less chance of losing this one. This one was a natural pregnancy; these things are always happy. My excitement just grew. My love for my unborn child exploded in my heart. I would wake up in the morning and feel like I was glowing from my heart outwards. I started thinking about when this baby would be born. I looked forward to maternity leave, I was fed up at work and could not wait for a bit of a break. I even looked through my wardrobe for some looser clothing I could wear to hide my initial bump.

I was so excited, I would will my bump to grow. I would look, profile, straight on, nothing yet. On the train home from work, after the station where everyone gets off and I can finally get a seat, I would sit and hold my tummy, talking to the baby inside my head, and continue during the whole 25 minute walk home. I spoke in French, I always wanted to speak to my children in French, just like my mum had done with me, so that they too would be able to communicate with my family in Switzerland. That Christmas I would be a mum! I would finally have my family. I could go spend Christmas with my wider family and not feel like a spare part. At last I felt, my value, my worth, my reason for being would be achieved. This was my calling and finally I could take my rightful place in the world, as the mum I've always known I was.

From the day I knew I was pregnant this little life was my baby. I had planned when it was due, when I could go and visit my mum, before I wasn't allowed to fly anymore. I planned what I would do in any time between maternity leave and having the baby. I hoped to work to the very last minute so I could spend as much time as I could with my baby. I never really understand people who want a few weeks off to 'get ready' for the baby. I suspect these people haven't ever waited as long as I have for the chance to spend time with their baby. This baby was so precious, I was going to spend every possible minute I could with it, even when it cried and I couldn't sleep for months, it was finally there, it was alive, it was mine. I had counted out the 12 weeks and then every month after that in my calendar and circled the dates.

I was thinking about how to make the announcement, not long to go and we could be official. This was my rainbow baby (born after the loss of a previous baby). I had seen some really sweet rainbow baby announcements. I thought this could be my re-entry into social media, my own good news story, my own happy family shot.

7th February 2015

I still can't believe it's real, you are real, after all this time waiting.

Especially days when symptoms aren't as bad. I wonder if I'm imagining it, almost like you are too good to be true, I don't deserve this, but it's not about deserving, it's just life. Life finally happening, to me!

I went into town, walking past Mothercare and Next, so excited that soon I'll be going in there to get things for you. I can't wait. On the bus back, I got really worried, we stopped in traffic, I was sat at the back and the bus shook so badly. I was so scared that you would be shaken free, I'm still so worried about losing you. I didn't know what to do, whether to get off the bus. Is a bit of vibration an issue? I'm not the only pregnant woman to ever get the bus, it's not like there are warnings about public transport. I'm over-reacting. I just want to keep you safe.

One morning, I started spotting. Nothing bad, so I tried not to panic, but I'd not felt pregnant the last few days. I was 10 weeks pregnant, I was almost over the dangerous period. I had been trying to stay positive. A couple of times I'd even asked Paulo if he thought I definitely was still pregnant? He told me of course I was. I would then feel bad that I had doubted the fact, like I didn't believe in my baby. I tried to call the midwife six times that day, no answer and again the next day. I finally got through to someone who told me I should head to the EPU Unit at the hospital, but that I'd need a referral from A&E first.

I went into hospital alone, first to A&E to get the referral, where I explained my symptoms to the doctor who saw me and watched as she typed 'abortion' onto the screen. I felt like I stopped breathing. She must have noticed my expression because she then said she was not sure that is what it was, but she needed to write something. I couldn't unsee it though. She was a professional, she obviously thought that's what it was. I think I knew it too, deep-down. How could I maintain any kind of hope at that point? I wanted to scream, but just gave her a weak smile. She then sent me onto the Early Pregnancy Unit, which I walked into in a daze. I was taken into a room and given a scan.

They confirmed there was no heartbeat. Those words. I felt a sense of panic overwhelm me. How? How can there be no heartbeat? Where was my baby? No! I felt all the air leave my lungs; my blood ran cold. NO! I was told that the size of the foetus was smaller than you'd expect at 10 weeks and that it had stopped developing roughly two weeks ago. I was dazed. How could this happen again? I drove home sobbing, barely able to see the road. My heart felt like it was breaking out of my chest, I almost wished it would, to relieve the pain I felt in it.

I told my boyfriend and he came home to be with me. My uterus felt really heavy, I constantly felt like everything was dropping inside me. Part of me willed the miscarriage to happen immediately, because it hurt too much to keep carrying my baby that was no longer there, another part of me felt that if I could just hold on to it, everything would be ok. They must be wrong. I loved my baby, I was protecting it, it was safe. Wasn't it?

That evening I lost my baby. There is no pain like it. And the awful shame, of having to flush away a baby that I am supposed to love and protect. I had been unable to keep my baby safe, the one thing a mother should do. I didn't want him to let go; I didn't want to not have him inside me anymore. I sat on the toilet and cried, pleading with him not to go. Crying out loud to my baby, "don't go!" I bled continuously from 10pm to 3am. I could barely leave the toilet in that time, because there is no way of controlling it and pads wouldn't last five minutes at that rate of flow. At about 3am, when the blood flow was starting to ease up, I sat on the sofa, exhausted, broken and empty. I felt like a shell, like the whole of me had fallen out into the loo. I found my favourite childhood film on television, the Breakfast Club. It felt familiar and comforting to have it on, but I couldn't concentrate on it, in the cold and dark living room. I just stared. I am not sure I will ever be able to watch it again. When the film ended, the flow had slowed even more, I felt confident enough to go to bed. I crawled in, hoping I never had to move again.

The painful cramps lasted the whole day Friday and started to ease up towards the end of Saturday. I sobbed, a lot, but the rest of the time I was completely numb. Like I wasn't really there. Paulo tried so hard to be there for me, but I felt so disconnected to life, to reality. How had my baby just gone? Vanished. Erased. Pregnancy just happens right? I know babies can die once they are born, through illness or accidents, but my baby was inside me. I was protecting it. I had done everything right, given up all the good stuff, the cheese, the wine. I was even crossing the roads at official crossings, not darting across between oncoming traffic. I had been so careful. How was my baby not there? I felt so empty, like there was nothing at all left inside me, no baby, no heart, no me, just a void filled with pain. On Monday I contacted the midwife to let her know that I no longer required our appointment.

I went back into the office on Tuesday. It took everything I had to not cry on the train in. I avoided any chat with anyone as I couldn't bare the mundane daily chat, I couldn't bring myself to smile. Nothing felt important enough to care about, my baby was gone. I felt I was gone too. At lunch time, my boss, the only person who knew what had happened, asked me how I was, that was too much, and I started to cry. She took me aside and told me that I needed to take all the time I needed, that I may feel ok physically but that I had lost a little life and all the hopes and dreams that went with it. It felt so nice for someone to acknowledge this. It was already such a huge part of my future, before it ever even was. It was part of me. It felt so hard to let go. I didn't want to. I worked from home for the rest of the week.

18th February 2015

I miss being pregnant. I miss the sore boobs, the exhaustion, the hope, the love. I miss my baby. This is so unfair. Miscarriage has to be one of the most painful things, all the pain, no baby, just emptiness. I was so close. Part of me wants to just curl up and let the sadness flood me. Nothing feels important, not work, not anything.

I had to go back to the Early pregnancy unit, where I sat amongst the happy pregnant women. They confirmed the miscarriage was over. I knew that. They also told me that since I'd had two miscarriages, I was more likely to miscarry again, on top of my age, which increased chances of miscarriages. So now, do I try again and face the possibility of a heart-wrenching and painful miscarriage? Of course. I have no choice, I keep going.

Why, every time I see a doctor, do I get more bad news? Surely statistically I'm due some good news? I'm due an appointment that doesn't send me home in tears. I just want to cry. All the time. My heart hurts. There's a lump in my throat, a weight where my heart should be. An internal scream creating such pressure I feel I can't breathe.

For a brief moment

For a brief moment, you were there
The shortest time
But I felt you
I loved you
Our story together is the shortest
Waiting for you had been the longest
Losing you was the most pain I'd ever
felt
Not having you is the hardest thing to
live through

February 2015

30th March 2015

I am ok most of the time now, but I feel my heart is broken underneath. Every now and then it comes up to the surface and I feel so desperately sad and life feels so incredibly unfair. I sometimes wonder if I have any part of my heart left unbroken? Still, I am fighting on and staying hopeful I'll get pregnant again. I will have you. I wanted that baby to be you. I wanted that baby. I'm so disappointed, I wanted to have my children a decade ago, I have missed out on 10 years of your life. 10 years of playing with you, 10 years of watching you sleep, eat, doing your laundry, loving you.

I started to bounce back, with a positive view that third time would work. Everyone knows third time is lucky. The saying has to come from some truth, right? I now knew I could get pregnant naturally, the doctors had been wrong about that. Maybe they were also wrong about my chances of another miscarriage being more likely. I also found out you were more fertile straight after a miscarriage, so no time to lose. Paulo and I planned a trip away to Bruges to cheer ourselves up and I had a spa weekend lined up with a girlfriend. I kept very busy, made lots of plans to catch up with various different friends. Not having any time to think has become a bit of a crutch of mine over the years. In April I found out I was pregnant again. I was overjoyed but also cautious.

12th April 2015

My period was due at the start of April, it didn't come, so I took a test. I am pregnant again! I am so excited but very scared too. Another few weeks and I may feel reassured. I am trying to take things easy but had four late nights last week. It's meant to be the most exciting time and I feel like I can't let myself believe it. I know you're there. I feel like me again.

I had told close friends about the miscarriage, so I felt there was no need to keep this new pregnancy a secret from them, they'd find out anyway, if it all went wrong. This time around I felt really sick, from the day I missed my period, every day. This felt like a really, really good sign. This was it. What was even more perfect is that this baby would be due just before Christmas, my favourite time of year, but also, recently, the most painful. I would still be a mum for Christmas this year. I would also be a mum before I was 40, which had always been my line beyond which I would not cross.

I was back on the app, looking at how big my baby was, in comparison to various foods, a sesame seed, a current, an olive, a strawberry, a lemon. What was developing this week? What would happen next week? When would I be able to take my maternity leave? I'd already been writing a few names down over the last couple of years, and when I thought of a new one, I would add it to the list.

It was my mums 80th in May and I was terrified of needing to fly when so newly pregnant, but I could not miss my mum's birthday. I researched flying when pregnant and it was all fine, all except the colossal amount of adrenaline that would be pumped around my body because of my fear of it. I still blamed myself for the last two miscarriages, I must have done something wrong, I didn't want to set one foot wrong this time. At least I wouldn't be flying alone, which always helps stem the fear. Besides, by the time the flight was due I would be almost 12 weeks, so pretty much out of the danger zone, it would be fine.

The Early Pregnancy Unit gave me an eight-week scan just to reassure me, ahead of my 10-week dating appointment. I went along by myself, as Paulo was looking after his niece and nephew that morning. The sonographer was very kind and appreciated I must be nervous since I'd had bad news last time I'd been there. I was impressed by his consideration. He placed the scanner and the screen flickered into focus. I held my breath. I could see a shape and a flashing white spot, which I was told was a very strong heartbeat. I tried so hard not to, but tears rolled down my face. Happy tears. Relief. There he was, my baby and he was fine. I was given a picture to take home and was so proud to have it. My little bean. I positively flew home on such a high. I had read that if there is a strong heartbeat at eight weeks, your chances of a miscarriage drop to less than five percent. That is extreme, no one is that unlucky, certainly not me. 95% chance this baby was making it. Those are excellent odds and I flew high on them.

5th May 2015

I saw you today, you were beautiful. I could see your little heart beating and I was so proud. The sonographer said it was a strong heartbeat. My little fighter. I love you. I cannot wait to hold you close. I cannot wait for our amazing life together to start.

Every week was a bonus. I'd read what was happening during that week, what size the baby was now. And so, my baby grew. I'd also take a sneaky peek at the following week and possibly the one after, but never more than that. I still had the books I had found in January sitting in my Amazon basket, waiting to be purchased. I didn't like to. Odd, since I'm not remotely superstitious, but it felt presumptuous to buy a book for something I had no evidence would actually happen and having those books if it didn't, would be too heart-breaking.

I felt so connected to this baby. I talked to him, again in French. I remember walking home from work one day and the moon was out, I winked at it, like I had the best secret in the world. Like I was the luckiest person in the world. I'd listen to calming music on my way into work, to not let the angry commuters disrupt my perfect little bubble of joy.

The dating appointment with the midwife felt monumental. I had actually made it to see the midwife. This was real. She asked all about my partner and I and our family medical background. I told the midwife that I had stopped feeling as sick that week and she said it's quite common for the nausea to stop around 10 weeks. I felt a little calmer then, if a professional says its ok, it must be.

Carried badly

The time came for the 80th birthday party, we flew over. That day I noticed I did not feel pregnant, perhaps it was because of the fear of the flight taking over my emotions? I can't describe what felt different. It must be linked to the hormone levels. All I know is that I have felt pregnant very soon in my pregnancies, usually a week before its time to take the test. I feel vibrant and alive, I felt complete. Its very difficult to describe. Now I no longer felt that.

The preparations were full on, shopping, cleaning, preparing, the days flew by. My mum gave me a very cute cuddly dog that she had called Patch, for the baby. I told her it was too soon for this kind of thing, but really, it's only a week away from announcement time, so its fine really. I know that she was so excited to be able to buy it and be able to give it to me.

Although I never felt any pressure on behalf of my mum to have children, I knew she desperately wanted to be a grandmother. I could see how she was with my cousins' children, she wanted to be part of that world and I was filled with guilt about her having to wait this long. I was heartbroken myself that she would no longer be the grandmother I had hoped, it would not be possible for my mum to babysit my child or have them stay over as I did with my grandma.

The party was on Sunday. The day was beautiful and sad. My mum was very unwell. There was tension amongst the family, which led to some members not being there. I was saddened by it, but glad they weren't there. When people can't see their part in something, you can't explain it to them, so distance was best for all, but an 80th birthday is such a big deal, especially with how ill my mum had been at the time. It felt like this could be the last birthday she would see. However, nothing could detract from the warmth of those who were there. My mum felt so loved and appreciated and finally accepted that she needed to go into hospital, after not eating properly for months.

The following day we flew back home then that week I travelled up to Halifax for an event with work and everyone went out for drinks the night before. One lady noticed I wasn't drinking and whispered, "you're not?" I could only grin, saying no after that was futile. I confirmed I was and had my 12-week scan booked for the start of the following week. That week I was asking my partner if he could feel my stomach getting more solid, since all the websites stated it would start happening now. I no longer felt the same and I was looking for signs that everything was ok. If only there was a window to see in and check on your baby, like with an oven.

On Saturday I met a friend from university and again, he said something which led me to grin, I couldn't help it I was over the moon and although I was officially 12 weeks, I wanted to wait for the scan to really believe I was out of the danger zone. He was really pleased for me. That evening I got home and there was a spot of blood. I knew.

There was more blood the following morning but Paulo kept telling me it meant nothing, I went along with that, but I knew. I couldn't feel my baby, my connection. I no longer felt whole. I hadn't felt pregnant enough over the last week. The only way I can describe this is that when I was pregnant, I felt complete, physically. A bit like, if you have an empty windowsill and you put a plant there and it looks so much better, the space comes alive, as if it was always supposed to have that plant. That's how I felt when I was pregnant, everything was finally just right. I felt so much more alive. Like a cloudy filter had been removed from my eyes, I could see more clearly. I felt that this was always how I was supposed to be.

We went to A&E and the doctor there did a scan, where she very kindly said "I'm sorry sweetie, there's no heartbeat". I felt like my heart stopped. It felt like it had dropped right out of my chest. No air could get into my lungs. The room caved in around me. I knew what she would say and yet still I felt myself crumple, like someone had removed all my bones. Inexplicable feelings of intuition in my mind are down to something tangible. Maybe its again just a hormonal flux that I was aware of, which was translated into a feeling of 'knowing' things weren't right.

My boyfriend came in to hug me and I held on tight, hoping that the pain could be squashed out of me. I knew I had to stop crying before it got uncontrollable. I felt a scream building up inside, with so much force behind it, I had to shut off my emotions because I thought I'd never be able to reign them in if they got out. I couldn't behave normally and feel the full force of what I knew was there. I managed to control myself to the state of just tears rolling down my face. Those I could not stop.

I then had to go up to the Early pregnancy unit, for them to confirm this, I don't remember this really. I know we went there; we'd have sat in the waiting room with all the pregnant women. They confirmed that the baby had stopped developing one-two weeks ago. I had known, I had sensed something, but the midwife had assured me it was normal. I was angry she'd not checked more. Just the assumption that once you are pregnant, then a baby will follow. That said, there is nothing she could have done. A miscarriage cannot be stopped. The doctor asked if I wanted a D&C (the baby being surgically removed) or to let things happen naturally. I felt it was better to happen naturally, since an anaesthetic is always a concern.

We drove home in silence. What was there to say? I got home and cried and yet still I was reserved. I didn't dare fully open the hatch to my emotions, because I didn't think I could ever contain them. If I felt the full force then I thought it would break me. I didn't think I'd ever be the same again.

One per cent of women have three miscarriages (stats from the time of my miscarriage); One percent. How was that me? For once I didn't want to be special. I didn't want to be in the top percentile, or in a class of my own. I wanted to be bog standard, normal, an average woman. With a 99% chance of having a baby third time round. I was so angry, against the world, the universe, nature, my body. In that moment I hated every single woman who'd managed to have a normal pregnancy and a healthy baby. How was this fair? It wasn't fair. I knew that. Life isn't fair. I reminded myself that some people don't get the opportunity to even try for a baby, that is even less fair. But maintaining an objective view was impossible. I didn't care that there were people worse off. My baby had died, and my body had let it. My heart finally let out the full force of its scream. It's difficult to describe this, it screams with pain rather than sound, the pain is pushed out, like a sound is by lungs, but the heart just pushes out pain, but it's still a scream.

This miscarriage was horrendous. The egg-sac was a lot bigger than the two previous. I had felt it pass last time, so this was a couple of weeks growth on top of that. I waited for it to start, I wanted it to happen, I wanted this to be over whilst at the same time, once again willing my baby to not be dead. Hoping for a miracle. I avoided going to the toilet as long as I could, I tried so hard to keep my baby inside me, hoping this wasn't really true. I couldn't wait long, since I was bleeding quite profusely. Again, I begged my baby to not go, not to leave me. I cried. So much. Paulo tried so hard to support me, but having a miscarriage is a very lonely thing. There is nothing anyone can do. There is nothing either partner can really do for the other in that moment. He didn't want me to just be sat in the loo, but the blood flow was continuous, I didn't feel confident to sit down in the living room or go to bed. He moved the cushions off the sofa, so that I could have somewhere a little more comfortable but with easier access to the toilet.

The pain was unbearable. Like my soul was being ripped out of my body. I think my heart carried on its silent scream for the duration. I was taking double doses of double-dose drugs and they didn't touch it. My mind was empty for a lot of it, you just have to deal with the physicality of it, its relentless bleeding. And there is a lot of blood to contend with. It just doesn't stop. There is no option to stop or think. When the bleeding was more manageable and the pain eased up a bit, I just curled up. I never wanted to move again. We both hugged and cried, I actually think I howled because the emotional pain was so great, but the moments after the miscarriage are pretty blurred, I don't remember a lot of the days after.

1st June 2015

The miscarriage has begun. The pain is horrendous. I was so sure this time was you; I had all the healthy symptoms. I don't want to flush my baby away. I saw the beautiful little heartbeat. I was so sure that was your heart. It's only supposed to be a less than five percent chance of miscarriage after seeing a strong heartbeat at eight weeks. And only 1% of women lose three babies. The odds were so in your favour and yet here we are. Why me? I don't want this. I want to stop this. My baby. I'd do anything for you to stay, but it's too late, your beautiful little heart has stopped, and I think mine has too.

I took a couple of days off work and then worked from home. Having learnt from last time, I didn't go back into the office for over two weeks. I do remember the new Director, (my managers' manager) shouting at me over the phone. I had been supposed to co-ordinate some slides with some data. One of the teams had given me the wrong data, the figures weren't right. Nothing felt right in my world and I completely missed this detail; I just didn't have the brain power to deal with things that felt so mundane to me. She shouted at me like I was a petulant child asking for sweets. She didn't know why I was off, just that I was sick. Perhaps she thought I was slacking? I know my brain wasn't really with me those few weeks after the miscarriage. Part of me was shocked that one adult could treat another like this, part of me just didn't care, my baby was dead. I felt like I was too. Life felt so utterly empty.

Gone

I don't know how to hurt anymore
I can't believe it's happened again
My tiny baby, my long-awaited child
Gone

I don't know what to do with myself,
how to sit, how to stand
I sometimes feel the pain and it
cripples me

Most of the time it's not there nor am I
I feel vacant and numb
I cannot bring myself to think about it
About the Christmas I was going to
have
About the joy I was going to live
To nothing

There's an emptiness where you are
supposed to be
Where I am supposed to be
The anger overwhelms me
Why me?

Last time I could feel positive for the future
This time I cannot see past this
Last time only my heart shattered
This time my body is in pieces

I want everything back to normal
What is normal with no future, no hope?
I'd like to feel like me again
Who am I now?

Goodbye is so hard without a hello
Your tiny heartbeat was so strong
My beautiful little blob on the screen
I believed

Sometimes I open the door just a crack
To feel, to escape the grey numbness
The dark shadows of despair grab at me to get out
Maybe numb is better

June 2015

I was due to go back to the clinic, so they could confirm that the miscarriage was complete. I knew it was, I'd lived it. My boyfriend came with me and we sat and we waited with other women, some heavily pregnant, some had also bought their babies. Beautiful gurgles, even beautiful cries. My uterus lurched at every new-born sound. At one point one lady came to sit next to me with her pram. I couldn't look in their direction, Paulo saw my face and we moved seats pretty quickly. My heart did that silent screaming thing again. I ached. I wanted to run away from this toxic place with all its pregnant patients or new parents, sat there, in their smug little bubbles, taunting me. We went into the familiar scanning room, where I was told that there was no pregnancy. I had definitely needed to hear that!

After a couple of weeks, I was still bleeding and could just feel my uterus all the time. It felt heavy and almost like it was pulsing. It's just not an organ you are supposed to feel. I was struggling to concentrate on anything at work. All I could think about was my uterus. It was empty but felt so heavy. A few times I wondered if I'd actually lost my baby or if my baby was still there? I didn't feel pregnant.

Back to the Early Pregnancy Unit once again. What a slap in the face! Not the, 'Was Once Pregnant Unit', not the, 'Can't Keep A Baby Alive Unit', the Early Pregnancy Unit. I didn't belong there. Back into the waiting room full of pleased-as-punch pregnant ladies and, more often than not, a young child in tow. My heart did its silent scream of agony, whilst I tried to pretend I was a normal human, not a hollow shell. I was told it should stop soon and that I'd need to come back in a week, if it didn't stop. Another difficult week at work, I could barely think straight. I felt so awful. Tired, heavy, vacant. The bleeding didn't stop, for another week. So back I went. Back to wait with the pregnant women and babies. This time I was kindly told there were probably still some 'elements' of the pregnancy remaining, which I would need to have surgically removed. So eloquently put. I was then referred for surgery.

The surgery date was a week later. This involved a lot of waiting. We both sat in the waiting room, silently watching other couples come in and then leave. Finally, we were called in. I had my surgery, it was very quick, apparently no more than 30 mins. Back in the recovery room, a young woman opposite was complaining about some cramps. I remember thinking, matey, the hard work has been done, your uterus is empty, these cramps are nothing in comparison to during. However, I suspect she didn't know. I suspect she'd opted for surgery rather than wait around for it to happen. Such a wise choice really, in hindsight. I wondered if it was a miscarriage or maybe it was an abortion?

12th July 2015

Yesterday evening for the first time in weeks, I felt like me again, Paulo said I was my 'feisty' self again. I realise, now that I can no longer feel it, that my uterus had been throbbing over the last few weeks. The hospital said I'd gone into shock, which is nice when I was told to just go home and come again a week later at the EPU. No wonder I felt so rotten! I think we may need to wait a while this time before trying again. I don't know what to do for the best. I just want to be pregnant again. I want to pick up where we left off. I want to have my baby. But I wanted THAT baby. I loved my baby. I feel so alone without you.

The doctor in A&E had said "by all means get a referral, but I'd try again ASAP". She also said I could try half an aspirin, but warned that there could be dangers with that. I've been reading about this, sounds like a no-brainer.

I have also been reading about women's immune system attacking their own babies, the immune system is so busy protecting the baby, or maybe just protecting the mum, that it kills the baby. From everything I've read it appears that no one really knows very much about miscarriages.

A few days after the surgery, finally, I stopped bleeding. It had been five weeks since I lost my baby. I was exhausted. I'd felt like I couldn't move on, because the miscarriage hadn't actually stopped. My mind hadn't even started to think about processing this. I was still in disbelief. I was just waiting for the scan to confirm I could tell everyone that my rainbow baby was finally here. I'd even planned the announcement. I felt numb a most of the time. Then something would happen to trigger a wave of complete desolation.

One weekend in August, I had friends coming over and was tidying up. I found the little dog my mum had given me, Patch, she'd called him. Still in the same paper bag, still in exactly the same place I'd put him a couple of months ago. I hid him at the back of a drawer. I couldn't look at him, but I also couldn't get rid of him, he was evidence my baby had existed, not just to me, he'd existed in the world outside of me. He'd existed for my mum.

Meeting with friends had become increasingly bittersweet, I love all my friends so dearly, but I felt like I was just surviving on some other, broken plane. I was ashamed of my brokenness, ashamed of my failure to have become a mother. Ashamed that they were all in the adult world and I was in an in-between world. I felt so very disconnected to life.

15th August 2015

I wake up and for a split second everything is ok. Then the memories and thoughts tumble into my head like a waterfall. I'm supposed to be on maternity leave. I'm supposed to be having our first baby together in two weeks. I'm supposed to be having another baby in a few months. I'm supposed to be a mum to a one year old, my first Little Egg. The heartache seems to be getting more intense, the closer I get to the due date.

I get up to get ready for work, go through the motions, feed the fish, feed the cat, have a shower, behaving completely normally. Inside I'm screaming. So much that I almost feel a throat ache, like I'm hoarse from all the screaming. Except it's all in silence. It's all hidden.

I get on the train and fast forward the songs on my iPod to one that reflects my mood. The screaming inside continues. A lady with the fateful 'smug' badge walks past. Well bully for you, with your baby on board. Please don't get on my carriage, please don't. Not today, I don't have the strength today. Phew, she walks past.

Smiling feels like too much today. I know I will, soon as I'm at my desk, or sooner if I see someone I know. Spoke too soon, someone I know in the lift. Here I go,' normal' me into action.

Thankfully, the day goes well, no triggers, nothing to tip me over the edge. I managed to smile, talk and laugh with my work buddies as if I weren't cracking up inside. As the day goes on, I start feeling better. I am back to being hopeful and philosophical. I can try again, next time WILL work, and, in the meantime, I am alive, I have some really good buddies and we have such a good time. Then I come home. I'm supposed to have you here. It feels more real here. I miss talking to you on my way back from the station. I miss you.

The next unexpected surprise was when my first period after the miscarriage started. I bled profusely. I mean non-stop. I was changing a tampon every 20 minutes and still I managed to make a mess of my underwear. I was at work. Why do these things always happen whilst I'm at work? I had to head home. I got an appointment for the next morning at my doctors' surgery. The young doctor who saw me asked if I was definitely not pregnant, since this can sometimes happen? My heart skipped a beat, did he just say that? Could I be? The tiny little light of hope flickered into a slightly bigger flame. I had to supply a urine sample. I waited whilst he got his tester paper out of the drawer and dipped it into the sample. Maybe this was it? Turns out, I wasn't. I felt crushed. So much emotion in such a short space of time.

However, once this doctor had heard my history, he said I should be referred to a recurrent miscarriage clinic, since this was my third. Why had the EPU not told me this? Its as if they were unaware of miscarriages at that clinic and unaware that one person can have more than one. The waiting room arrangements are far from sympathetic, the fact they make you have a scan, then go back out and wait again before seeing the doctor, when you've just been told your baby has no heartbeat. Also, the fact that I had bled so much I'd gone into shock by the time I'd had the surgery, but I had been told to just come back the following week. Early pregnancy is when most miscarriages occur. Surely part of their remit is miscarriages and yet the knowledge and understanding about this seems limited. A recurrent miscarriage clinic sounded hopeful. I would finally know why. Next time, my baby would stay. Still, this was an NHS referral, so there was going to be a wait.

I was still in the thick of my grief. Everything was difficult. Getting up every day required a huge effort.

Even things like opening the post felt too difficult. I let it pile up. I did not have the headspace to deal with anything. I was numb most of the time, but the little thinking power I had, I needed to use to just go to work and act normal. Anything outside of that was surplus. I didn't call my mum as much as I should. I didn't talk to friends as much as I should have. I watched telly like it was just white noise with no picture. Nothing really went in.

Every now and then a sense of panic overcame me, a real sense of dread about my situation, like that feeling when you can't find your wallet and your blood runs cold. I felt so out of control. I usually managed on a day to day basis to drown out my emotions so I could function, knowing that if I should open that particular trap door, it would unleash untold monsters from the abys of my broken heart. I felt like I was in a nightmare, watching myself from above. Like I have to get a flight, the final call has been made and the doors are closed but I am sat motionless by the window of the departure lounge, watching it leave. I'm trying to stop it taking off without me, but I can't, it's out of my hands, I am powerless. Life was taking off without me. I was separated from it. My life was on hold, in this nightmare.

I am embarrassed to admit that in the weeks, possibly months following my last miscarriage, I was not always a nice person. One example, I had a seat on the train and a pregnant woman got on. Not heavily pregnant, but evident enough. I pretended not to see her, which I never do, I get up for anyone who seems more in need. As children my mum wouldn't let us sit on the bus if there were any adults standing, I still have that mindset. This time, I just remember thinking "if you get the baby, then I get the seat!" I know that was awful, but in that moment, I felt there was a kind of justice there, albeit I'd much rather have been stood and pregnant than have the blasted seat. I was just so angry.

I had no one to be angry with. I don't believe in god. For me, there is no such thing as destiny. I believe life happens and it is all about how you deal with it. It doesn't happen fairly. Pain is not spread equally amongst all. I have tried my hardest and done everything in my power to make this happen for me and not wait until it's too late. Yet still I found myself 39 and childless. The anger had to be directed somewhere, needed to be diffused and I found these little, petty releases, like hating anyone wearing the baby on board badge, kept me from losing the plot. I also directed a lot of that anger towards me. I'm the one who lost my babies. I'm the one who failed them. It's in the name. Miscarriage. Carried badly. My one job as a mother, to protect and I couldn't do that, even when they were safely in my tummy. The one thing every woman can do, and I couldn't. My confidence really took a beating.

I was trying to feel better, to find answers, to not feel so lonely. I looked online for developments and studies in miscarriages and found some books to read.

The research showed me that more than anything, it was still a very new field with few answers. I did read that Vegemite had been found to be successful in lowering miscarriage risk in mice. I bought some Vegemite. It did not taste good. I decided to wait until I was pregnant before I tried it again. I found many of the books lacked some depth, it was all about the happy ending. They also completely skirted over the grief and the crazy, which is the only way of describing the emotional rollercoaster and internal dialogue that was going on in my head. The crazy isn't constant, I'd go through days, even weeks of being absolutely fine and normal, but then, something would trigger the crazy and out it came, the heartache, the jealousy, the rage and I was left to squash these feelings. I usually did, but it usually took a couple of days to get back on track after a set-back.

I have since realised that my jealousy isn't so much resenting what others have, but resenting what I don't have. Jealousy may feel like its directed at others, but I think it's really about your own self-esteem, your lack of acceptance at the status quo. It's about life experience and the status these give, or deny you. There is a status in being a mum. Its a privilege, a success. Those who just get motherhood without a battle, possibly don't even realise this. Those who don't have it, feel it. Or certainly I do. I really feel acutely aware that I'm not in the club.

Generally, there isn't really a great deal of information out there. The reading material I was given at the IVF Clinic was scientific; what procedures they carry out; what they do with any 'waste' products etc. There was no aftercare or sympathy after my first miscarriage at the Fertility clinic. There was none at the Early Pregnancy Unit and yet the A&E doctor had been so kind. Infertility and struggling to conceive are still almost taboo subjects and miscarriage is all but hidden. Again, the reading materials are mainly scientific, along with information about the miscarriage association. People do not talk about it, it's painful, emotional and can be traumatic. Perhaps also because it feels like a failure. Potentially, the fact that most women who have a miscarriage do then go on to have a baby means that miscarriages may not have the same negativity to the majority. The loss of the baby is the same but there is no loss of identity. Motherhood is still achieved.

However, when you lift the lid on it, it seems far more frequent than you would expect. I do find the statistics confusing, there are lots of facts about one in four, some say one in four women have a miscarriage, others say one in four pregnancies end in miscarriage. They are very different. I think women like me skew those numbers.

7th September 2015

My sorrow for the babies I have lost seems to be never ending, the future I was meant to have, the me I was supposed to be now. The Christmas I was supposed to have this year, twice! I'm going through several phases at once. I still feel shocked and numb, in complete disbelief that this has happened again. But I still want a baby, I want to carry on from where I left off. My periods are still all over the place and irregular. Having got pregnant so quickly after the miscarriage in February, I assumed it would happen again. It isn't happening.

My life wanting a child feels very selfish sometimes, my pain, my desire for a baby that feels stronger than everything else. It's all about me. Except it's not just about me, there are other things at play, my relationship with a man who wants children, at what point would his desire for a child become more important than our relationship? My place in society, the one I want to have as a mother, later a grandmother. There are expectations from society about when you should have a family, if you're going to have one (obviously some chose not to).

There is also the continuation of the species, a normal biological response to hormones and also a deafening biological clock. Besides, when I look at others' lives, they are equally consumed by their own worlds, about their families, situations or careers, orchestrating family life and being exhausted by it. The headaches caused by normal life. People all care most about what they care most about. That is just good time management.

There was no let up from my grief. Every now and then I did feel like me again. Just me. Here. Now. Busy at work, trying to forge a career, making sure the bills are paid, trying to not get soaked in the rain, just normal plodding on. I was still training as a Counsellor and Psychotherapist in the evenings, but had also been enjoying what I was doing at the bank, working on projects. I hadn't had any formal training as a Project Manager, but the last few years had been involved in delivering progressively larger projects. It felt nice, to just be normal, to be me. I appreciated the luxury of being me, of being neither numb nor raw with pain. This must be part of my new, chilled me. The one who takes everything in her stride because it's out of your hands anyway. I sensed that it was a fragile state, the bubbling emotions seemed to never be far from the surface, since they were so easily triggered, but I did appreciate these moments.

I tried to live in the now. I wanted to feel like me again, I wanted to bounce back. I had lost my babies, but in the process also lost me. I was heartbroken, but still so grateful, I had a good life, I earnt well and never had to worry about food, or being safe. I had a beautiful garden and a little house, with such a cosy and friendly feel. I had a wonderful guy who I really, really loved. I felt so lucky. And the icing on the cake, or the cherry on top of the icing, is that I had the most sweet-natured cat. I felt so lucky that I was the one who got her. Anyone could have gone to that shelter. We were meant to find each other. I was extremely lucky that day, to find my little love and to all intents and purposes my surrogate baby.

It was nice to find this balance. I guess you do slowly get used to a loss and build your life without the one you've lost. In my counselling training I learnt about the Tonkin Grief model and this felt like it. The model says you don't get over a loss, you learn to live with it and a new life gets built around it, to incorporate it. Like all grief, it never fully disappears, but you get used to a new life. Is this also how you get the women who can say "I couldn't have children"?

Much like to my reaction to the story on the infertility website last year, I found this kind of acceptance frightening. I didn't want to accept this and simply move on. I needed to fight it, I needed to know I was doing all I could. Perhaps I was prolonging my own pain, creating it even? It would be easier to accept. To stop fighting nature. She had a larger army than me. Again though, much like the article of the lady whose heartache emerged again as her friends became grandmothers and she could not, I do not want to find myself in that position. One of passive-aggressive resignation to the status quo. No, I would not stop fighting for my part in life, my role as a mum.

14th September 2015

This has almost become a new battle in this war of mine. Between finding inner peace and fighting for a cause I really believe in, fighting for the life I want, not just accepting the one I have.

Martin Luther King said something along the lines of, 'when you stop fighting against what is wrong, then you stop being alive'. I know he meant serious matters such as discrimination. But this situation is wrong. I am supposed to be a mum. It feels so wrong that I am not. I am not who I should be. This is probably the polar opposite to what the Dalai Llama would say. Well in this instance I'm with Dr King.

Stuff inner peace. I want crazy disorder, a pile of washing the size of an elephant, sleepless nights, sticky marks on windows, toys everywhere, days since I last had time for a shower. Most importantly, a tiny little body, snoozing peacefully in a cot. The little chest, in the cutest babygrow slowly moving as the teeny lungs breathe in and out. The sleepy grumbly little noises of a contented baby. My baby. You.

How am I still waiting? How have all my efforts not worked out? How have I had to lose three babies? One could have stayed, surely? Why weren't they you?

I just went out to get a sandwich today. In front of me a very small little girl, in the cutest little raincoat was standing in awe at the lights under the Clink Street bridge. Her mum waited for her ahead and she ran to catch up and slid her tiny hand into her mums' outstretched hand. My heart dropped, a lump formed in my throat and tears stung my eyes. Such a simple gesture so often ignored and taken for granted. I would do anything to feel that. To hold *my baby's hand. Your beautiful little hand.*

The big 4 - 0

So much of normal life is disrupted when trying to get pregnant. Your calendar is now blocks of 'trying to be'; 'could be' and 'am not'. In the 'trying to be' block, you need to ensure you are home and together often enough to be doing the 'trying'. You are taking your folic acid and trying to be healthy. I needed to plan ahead with regards to visits to my mum's or weekends away with friends, no easy task since these things are generally planned months in advance and my periods had not been as regular since the last miscarriage.

In the 'could be' block, you go into super protective behaviour, no caffeine, none of the foods which are not permitted or could be an issue. I drank a lot of water, as its encouraged. I avoided people who were ill and tried to ensure I had no late nights planned. I also used to try to walk a little slower, I'm usually rushing around, zipping between slow-walking tourists around London Bridge, running between moving traffic to cross a road.

In these weeks I started to be more careful. I would also not do things like mow the lawn, just in case.

The 'am not' block was a tough time emotionally and would often consist of last-minute plans to get out and do something as a distraction.

23rd September 2015

Unfortunately, my next ovulation falls right when I'm away, so another month lost. I had not bought these tickets with that in mind. I can't remember now if I was still pregnant when I booked these, I think I was, so obviously that was not a consideration. I'm usually so good at planning around my monthly cycle, so we can try in the middle of it. Still, it means I can chill out this cycle. Drink alcohol eat Pate and cheese and not think about it at all. Likely!

I am really struggling at the moment. I'm not sure if it's just the baby thing, or the time of year, mornings (and evenings) getting darker etc. I am so sick of life being the same. The repetition of my cycle, of my emotions. Of feeling like my life is on hold until that moment when it all comes together, and I can be a mum. But that is not how it would be. It would then be an endless cycle of nappies and sleepless nights. So still drudgery, just not the same. I guess the difference is, there is an end in sight to the sleepless nights, they are certainly shorter lived than my wait for motherhood. At the moment, I cannot see an end to my childlessness.

One thing I found now, was that my body was playing tricks on me. All three pregnancies I'd had, I had felt twinges early on, I'd had a severe migraine, I had felt pregnant. I started getting really hot overnight and remembering a lot of dreams, which is very unlike me, normally I'd remember a dream every other year at most. However, after my third miscarriage, these things started to happen just before my period was due. That along with the fact that for a good six months after the third miscarriage, my periods were very irregular, meant that my hopes were raised far too often and came crashing back down, adding to my existing feelings of failure and heartache.

In hindsight I think I was still very numb from it, but I remember feeling that I was trying not to think about babies or pregnancy at all. I felt that I could not remain at the same level of heartache. Life is far too short. I often thought of my beautiful friend who had died two years before already, she had also wanted to have children so I felt that even the hope of a child is a gift, the opportunity of trying for one and I really wanted that to be enough to make me feel grateful. I felt awful when it wasn't.

19th October 2015

Last week was a tough week. Thursday, a friend of mine sent a message to say she was thinking of me and the babies I'd lost. It was Baby Loss awareness week 9-15 October and Thursday was Baby Loss awareness day. I should have read the message at home, had I known. I had to run to the ladies and cry. I was so pleased that someone remembered my babies. I never held them or even felt them kick, but I loved them, and I think of them and the fun we should be having every day.

I never know what will trigger me. On Friday, I went to pick up a Christmas cushion I'd ordered. This Christmas is going to be particularly tough, so I thought I'd over-compensate with more decorations. The online pick-up area is right at the back of the shop, slap bang in the middle of the new baby section. All these beautiful, tiny babygrow's, toys and blankets, that I should be using, just taunting me, as I walk past, to pick up a freaking cushion I've bought to try to provide the expected Christmas cheer to my home, without the baby I'm supposed to have.

I felt like I was dragging my heart through barbed wire instead of soft Babygrow's. I wanted to run home and hide in the very depths of my bed, until the pain stopped. My legs felt like they'd collapse under me; I felt all my strength drain out of my limbs. It took everything I had to act normal and not break down. I then walked back to the office and continued the day as if nothing strange happened. It's exhausting.

Then Saturday I received a letter from the local Health Visitor. Apparently, I am due a baby on the 18th December and they want to discuss my pregnancy and future parenthood plans with me. It felt like I'd been winded. How is that allowed to happen?

I have been treated at the Early Pregnancy Unit and my local doctors' surgery have referred me to the recurrent miscarriage clinic. I have had scans, blood tests, surgery AND have not seen the midwife since I was 10 weeks pregnant in May. How did this letter slip through?

Whilst I was lost in my internal world of hurt and trying to find a way back to me, I was facing another challenge at work, which really tested my determination to remain happy and see the positives. The organisation went through a period of lowering staff numbers, otherwise called 'realising benefits'. Everyone had to apply for their own jobs again, only there were less jobs than people. I had been on secondment with a team for over two years, but because of what was going on outside work, I had not tried to make this a permanent move, I don't remember now if the opportunity of a permanent role had even been available in that time, I don't actually think so. In the meantime, the department where I was deemed a permanent employee had been disbanded, the separate teams had all gone their own ways and new management had joined, so there was nowhere for me to return to and no one in management who knew me. In these scenarios, you can only apply for a role within your 'permanent' team. For me, this would have been the role and team that no longer existed. I had to apply to my previous department, where no one knew me and therefore were obviously going to pick the people whom they had been working with over the last few years. So, I ended up being made redundant.

I had a few months before the redundancy would start and I could still apply for roles within the organisation. I applied for a few, I got through to interview stage, but I didn't get them. This was a huge blow, I felt rejected and embarrassed. My confidence was not in a good place. I already felt like a failure because I had not been able to keep my babies alive. One of my interviewers told me afterwards that it was clear that I could do the job and that my responses to the questions were well thought out.

I didn't know what to think of that. Does that mean it was just me they didn't like? Did they already have someone lined up for the job but had to go through the motions of interviewing others? Perhaps they could see that my fight was gone. Maybe, because my grief was so thinly disguised under my 'office face'. Or maybe simply because I didn't really want any of the jobs I applied for. What I really wanted was to be on maternity leave, with my baby, so maybe my lack of enthusiasm came through? Either way, I took it personally as a reflection of my already very fragile self-worth. What a build up to Christmas this year was!

The next diary entry was not written to my child, which now looking back I'm not sure why. I know that I felt very distant from ever becoming a mum and perhaps this entry is a reflection of this.

6th November 2015

Well, more weird goings on, my period is now six days early this month. It has never done that before. one or two days yes, but six? What is going on? Least the flow is normal again. The crushing despair as I see my period starting is so difficult to pick myself up from. Having ever been pregnant feels like a dream, a different lifetime. A different person.

I hate not having any power or control over this. I'm a very determined and proactive person, but this is out of my hands completely. I can't work harder at it; I can't make more or better eggs. I can't make my body get pregnant. Or stay pregnant. I hate that. I can't think my way out of this. I can't fight for this. I can't learn anything to take forward and improve the situation for myself. I can't train my uterus to work better.

It is so unfair. I want to be angry, but with who? I was supposed to be a mum in my 20's. How has this happened? I still can't believe that I have no baby at the end of this year.

I have tried so hard to keep thinking positively, in the hope that the universe colludes to make it so. I am eating well, hardly drinking anything these days. I have tried not thinking about it at all, not really looking at my monthly cycle other than keeping tabs on my periods which have been so random since the last miscarriage. I'm not thinking about it and I mean, really not thinking about it, not just, not talking about it. I have pushed the thought right out of my mind. It's been quite easy this last month, since I have been placed at risk of redundancy, so I have been entirely engrossed in thinking about work. But not thinking about it hasn't worked either. It seems that nothing, really nothing I do or don't do makes the slightest bit of difference.

This is hard for me to accept. I am someone who finds solutions, who when faced with a problem finds a way out. I have perseverance, I have resilience and I have determination. None of that matters here. So, what can I do? I need to feel I'm doing something.

What is worse is that it's my fault, I waited too long to start the IVF. I foolishly hoped I might find love still, or if I was dating someone, that it might go somewhere. I regret that. I had been thinking about and planning on having a baby for so long. I needed to save which slowed me down too. Maybe I should have just had a one-night stand. But how would I explain that to a child? I couldn't say it was a mistake, it would have been premeditated. Besides, now I know that wouldn't have worked with my endometriosis.

I keep thinking I should start the adoption process. I don't want to start that in a couple of years' time, to then have to wait another couple of years or more to pass the process. I can't start being a mum at 45. I was supposed to be a young mum!

Many friends who had struggled to get pregnant had spoken to me about their heartache or nervousness. My inner therapist loved the fact that I was trusted and that by talking about what I'd been through, it had opened up the conversation for others. I was glad I could support my friends through what was always, regardless of circumstances, a heart-breaking journey. However, I also watched as each went on to have a at least one, often two children since we'd talked. In my head, their concerns and worries, followed by the arrival of their baby just emphasised how separate and useless I was, because every one of them had gone on to have a child. Every single one.

Once again, I felt so disconnected to real life. I was just watching from my usual spot behind the glass barrier unable to fully take part. Why not me? Why did I deserve to go through this? It was becoming a running joke between my boyfriend and I, how everyone, regardless of their circumstances ended up with children before me. A painful joke, which only served to destroy my confidence and hope, a hope I was fighting so hard to keep hold of.

I found it increasingly hard to remain a good friend, whilst finding it so incredibly painful. It's like I had reached my threshold of babies and pregnancies I could cope with. I felt like I was the one in the wrong. I was the bitter one, the one who couldn't get life right, I couldn't begrudge the fact that everyone else was doing it right. Just living normal life. I tried to bury my hurt and be involved, but it became very difficult. I fought really hard against my pain. I really pushed for my hope to take over once again. I was determined to remain an active participant in life, in everyone's life. I wanted to get back to a sense of me. I didn't want this other side to me.

I recognise now with my work with bereaved clients that this was still grief. Everything is harder when you are grieving, but at the time I felt like this was my normal, I would remain in this endless loop of painful triggers. I couldn't see an end to it, try as I might to shake it off. Now I can see that even when I had an ok day, I was not ok. When you are grieving, you don't think one day you won't hurt so much. You can't imagine ever feeling any better about your loss. At the time I was still at college and training and had not yet started working with bereaved clients, but I think now, this has helped me with my own losses.

25th November 2015

Last weekend was the first free weekend in a long time. It was nice, I was able to sit and watch television, I hunted out cheesy Christmas films, I love them, my favourite time of year, with their families and happy endings, intertwined with Christmas adverts, all showing excited children and happy parents. It made me cry, but I was compelled to watch all the same. This

Christmas was supposed to be so different.

However, hope has mostly taken over again. I've let go of my own personal barrier of having to have had children by 40. I've accepted this won't happen and have stopped giving myself a hard time about it. I am also still focusing on appreciating all the things I do have. It's amazing how, if you are determined to change your thought processes and determined to see the positives, it does happen, but it feels like such hard work still. It will become easier I hope.

I've worked hard to find joy in life again. It's something I have to keep working at. I still have days when I feel like a lead weight walking through treacle, surrounded by a dense fog. Nothing in front, nothing behind, numb, empty and invisible. Those days are hard, especially when it's a working day and I have to act fine.

Perhaps this has meant that my feisty and slightly aggressive nature that loved the vitality of living in such a *huge and vibrant city has now diminished, or have I just mellowed with age? I embodied the city life, I worked hard and played hard. I had little patience of any kind really. I find that as I've worked hard on my wellbeing recently, I have lost that inner speed-demon and party animal. I enjoy simpler things. I am calmer. I find peace in gardening.*

Walking to the station this morning, there were the usual aggressive and selfish drivers around. Two separate incidents occurred where a driver beeped their horn for an unnecessarily long period of time. I don't need this. I don't want to be surrounded by so much anger and negativity, when I'm fighting so hard for the positive. I am having a tough time and yet determined to stay positive and happy, why should others be allowed to threaten that? I need calm. I possibly need to leave London. Did I really say that?

I remember going Christmas shopping, there is a huge Boots, which is a useful cut-through. We were just going through the shop and took the escalator down, just by the escalator, the baby section. I saw a little fleecy outfit and let out a loud sob before I could stop myself. I tried to style it out as a cough, but the tears kept flowing. My baby, my babies, were gone. My heart, my life was so empty. Paulo grabbed my hand and pulled me through to the other side of the shop, where I was able to shake myself back into reality. My childless reality. Come on woman, find the joy, its Christmas!

That Christmas I went back over to my mums. The usual feeling of having failed at moving forwards, failed to change my life. I watched my cousins with their children. I watched my mum. She had forgotten initially about my miscarriages, which had really hurt. The single most painful and defining moments of my life, forgotten. But her memory is not what it should be. It meant that I didn't talk to her about it any longer. Losing a baby hurts, especially if that baby isn't even recognised as a being, because to me they were so real, they existed. I felt them. I couldn't bear for them to be forgotten, or not acknowledged, I felt it made a mockery of my loss, which I felt very deeply.

2016 loomed. My birthday was a big number this year. 40. That meant something right? This would be my year! In the New Year, I had applied for an internal job and, after a telephone interview, got the job as a Business Change Manager. I would be working on a new Organisational Design for an area of the business (this would mean agreeing what the business area would look like in terms of its structure, improving the efficiency of what it's going to do and who is going to do it) and shaping the new Target Operating Model (how the business were going to achieve what they needed to do). See, this was my year.

Maybe it was seeing the hollow emptiness in my vacant expression which had put the others off? It was a fixed term role, after which I could either try to find another job or take the redundancy. The trouble was, it was based in Edinburgh and I was expected to go up there every week to start with, and then probably every other week. I so hate flying. So, there I was, trying to stay really cool and calm so I could get pregnant again, and having to face my worst fear, twice weekly.

As to trying, I only had a few days per month when I could actually get pregnant and since I only have one ovary, it was only every other month and I was now going to be away from home for three days a week, every week, for a while. How was that going to work? I was angry that I needed to make this choice, paying bills or having a family.

21st January 2016

This week has been so incredibly hard. My period started at the weekend, once I had yet again convinced myself that this month could be the month. I'd felt really hot, I had a migraine, and a couple of nights where I'd remembered my dreams. All my early pregnancy symptoms. This one was back to a normal length of time and I felt normal cramps too. Maybe my body did just need more time? Part of me is almost relieved I'm not pregnant, because I can't separate pregnancy from heartache. I'm not ready to face more.

A friend let me know she was pregnant. I had suspected. Partly that gives me hope, because she's been trying for some time. But at the same time, the bitterness has reared its extremely ugly head. She's almost a decade younger than me. Surely, it's my go first?

At college, one of the ladies described how she went through the adoption process and the minute they were approved; she fell pregnant. I really need something like that. To feel like I'm actually doing something, moving forwards. Taking action towards having you. I also need to just let go of some of the pressure to become a mum. I decided adoption would be great, *start the process and no doubt fall pregnant whilst doing it. I suggested it when I got home, he said no. I said I'd do it alone to which he responded, "well do it alone". That led to a couple of hours of silence between us both.*

The pain is still so raw, I need to do something. This birthday coming up is weighing on me too. I always knew I'd have my family by 40. I knew it. I now have three weeks left, and I have failed. I feel like I really need to be doing something. Anything.

My 40th birthday came and went. I hated it. I hated the fact that I still didn't feel I was alive, I was just treading water, waiting for my real life to start. I also hated the fact that I felt that way, I should be more appreciative of life. I tried so hard to celebrate and really mean it. I didn't. I felt hollow inside, but usually managed to pretend I was fine, with a decent smile and cheerful chatter.

However, that February I didn't get a period. I knew it would happen, of course it would, I'm meant to be a mum and maybe 40 being the cut off just meant, before 41. I took a test. Negative? That's weird, maybe the hormone levels were too low to show up still? I waited a couple of days, still negative. March, I didn't get a period either. I took another pregnancy test, still negative.

By now my uterus felt extremely uncomfortable. I was weirdly willing my period to come, since I didn't think I could get pregnant until it had, but also, because it felt too cruel to not have a period, but not be pregnant either. It was like my body was laughing at me. I was terrified my menopause had started. I ended up going to the doctors, more blood tests and scans. Nothing was coming up. The doctor asked if I was stressed? Grief of losing three babies in two years, stress of being made redundant, new job and weekly flights. No, everything is just peachy! At least I wasn't menopausal, which was a huge relief. After two and a half months, I finally had a period.

The bracelet

In May we went to see a fertility expert at Guys Hospital at London Bridge. He said we should start IVF straight away. Due to my low egg reserve he thought we may need to use donor eggs. I was heartbroken, I had had my own children, right there, safe and growing where they should be, and I lost them. I was hit with such a sense of loss again, for my biological children.

I'd already been told I may need donor eggs, but at the time I almost hadn't considered it a real likelihood, since we were still trying IVF with my eggs, so I hadn't emotionally connected with this idea. I had also since been told I couldn't have my own, therefore, I had faced this loss of a genetically related child already. But then I had been pregnant naturally, twice. How can the same loss hurt so much and still feel so fresh, so new, so raw? At the time, I felt like, if this was my only chance of having a child, then it's a no-brainer, of course we do that.

I thought ploughing on regardless was a normal reaction. Surely motherhood at whatever cost? I was reminded of a lady at work, who when she'd found out I'd done two rounds of IVF by myself and miscarried three babies, had told me that she had tried IVF once with her husband. It had failed and she had stopped there, unable to face another round. She still found it hard to not have had children. I wondered what made some women stop. It obviously wasn't that the desire for a child which had stopped. I struggled to understand this choice, I was filled with such a drive to be a mum that I would move any mountain to achieve it.

I think there is a lot of judgement for a woman's choice and reaction to the heartache involved in infertility. Possibly because it's never talked about. Only once you find out someone else has been through it, do we open up about our own journey. So those outside the niche group don't hear half the stories, don't know what led to any decision. I realised I too was judgemental. I thought once again to my dread of ever needing to say the words, "I couldn't have children", my refusal to accept the situation as it was, which may be prolonging my pain, my sense of failure as a woman. I was fighting so hard to feel joy in what felt like my half a life. Perhaps if I accepted, I wasn't going to have children and found other ways to feel fulfilled I would be happier? Maybe I am just keeping the wound open?

I contacted Lewisham, I was now in a couple, surely, I could get some help with the cost of IVF? Apparently not, since I was now 40, they only paid for couple where the woman was up to 39. Of course, they did. Were the making up the rules as I contacted them? Luckily, I had continued to save, since I had actually assumed we'd need IVF or some form of fertility treatment after being told I'd not carry my own. Always saving for motherhood. We'd been together two years and other than a couple of city breaks, had not had a holiday together. A baby was always my priority.

Around the same time, after several months, the appointment letter came through for St Mary's Recurrent Miscarriage Clinic in Paddington. Apparently one of the best. I went along to the first appointment to find that the Recurrent Miscarriage Clinic shared a waiting room with the Gynaecology Unit and that women who were pregnant came to both. I got to sit with pregnant ladies again. Oh, I had missed these encounters! That first appointment was slow, but I finally got to see a doctor and explained the journey so far. More scans and blood tests, they took A LOT of blood, I think 10 small vials. The nurse could see my face when she bought them in and joked, "you may as well get comfortable", she reassured me it was because they tested for everything, which I was reassured by. This would find out what was going on. I waited between the tests and scans, back in with the pregnant ladies.

I had to go back a couple of weeks later to discuss the initial results. They saw that I had a heart shaped uterus, which they felt could have caused the miscarriages. I was told I'd need surgery. The first appointment they could get was in November, with a potential surgery date in January. It was June. I was not allowed to try to get pregnant before this surgery. Tears stung in my eyes. I could not believe this.

Partly I was glad to have found out what the issue was, once this was removed, then I'd obviously be able to carry to term. But I'd not got pregnant in a year now, I was 40. Were they joking? How could I be expected to wait over seven months at my age? I was shocked. I couldn't hold the tears in. Turns out that was the best thing to do, because they called me back a few days later with a cancellation date, 17th August, even better, I'd have the initial appointment and the surgery all on the one date. Result. I felt like I was actually moving forwards. This would sort it. I could even be pregnant again before Christmas.

7th June 2016

Last week was tough. It was one year since I lost baby number three. The baby I was sure would be you. One year since nothing else has happened. One more wasted year of not being a family. One more year I have missed out on your life, on spending time with you. On the actual anniversary I found out another old colleague is pregnant, the following day I found out a friend was expecting her second. Of course she is. And I was also invited to someone else's baby shower. All the presents, the babygro's. You want me to sit and look at possibly the cutest thing and be excited that yet someone else gets to have their family and not me? I almost laughed, it's a joke. Motherhood is definitely haunting me.

My soul aches. I look at my beautiful garden in gorgeous sunshine and I can't crack a smile. The only thing which brings a tiny speck of joy back is my little Matilda.

This pain feels unbearable. Another part of me knows that people out there are suffering more, are dying, facing starvation, losing their loved ones, living somewhere unsafe, scared for their lives, or even no longer scared for their lives, but facing hopelessness. I have hope, I know I'll have you and love you, so why can I not stop this pain?

I wasn't happy about having surgery again. I'd been so distracted by work and the thought of more surgery, I realised in July that my period was late, by three days.

I waited another couple of days, then took a test and it was positive. I was terrified, I had a heart shaped uterus, I wasn't supposed to be getting pregnant until after the surgery. I was likely to miscarry. The next day, I started bleeding. This miscarriage was the easiest for me, I barely knew I was pregnant. This miscarriage wasn't anywhere near as painful as the others.

My first miscarriage had been around a similar gestation period and yet the pain had been unbearable, and the blood just didn't stop. This didn't feel like that, it did almost feel like a heavy period. It felt surreal. Had the test not been positive I'd never have believed it. I checked online and chances of a false positive are extremely unlikely. After such a long time of waiting, of hoping, of trying and here I was with a non-event miscarriage. I didn't really feel like I'd lost a baby this time. As horrid an experience as the last three miscarriages were, I felt the loss of my baby warranted feeling so much pain. It warranted being a traumatic experience, it acknowledged that something precious had died. This time I didn't feel like I'd been pregnant at all. I hadn't felt connected. Perhaps this was what is called a chemical pregnancy? Do they feel different? I may have just still felt numb from all the events over the last couple of years.

August 17th came. Due to a slight allergy to latex, I was told I'd be first into the theatre, so there would be no traces of latex there. They then decided against that and I ended up being last. So, having gone in at 7.30am, I went into surgery at 4.30pm. I'd had no food, no water, my head was pounding so badly, through dehydration I expect. It would have been a long wait anyway, but to have been told you'd be first and then go through last felt a bit cruel. I wanted to shout at them! I had to sign another disclosure because of what could go wrong. Apparently with this procedure, they fill your uterus with water, to check the shape of it, but you can die from this, because of the amount of liquid inserted. I didn't really take on board any danger to me, it was my only chance at a successful pregnancy, at motherhood. No question, I signed.

I had to go back to the Recurrent Miscarriage Clinic to discuss the results of my surgery. Back with the pregnant ladies in the waiting room. I tried not to look, but like when I was a child, I was drawn to look at the pregnant belly. I had the oddest sensation, like somehow my uterus was a magnet drawing the baby, I felt almost like the baby was in my uterus. It's a very strange feeling to describe. It's not pleasant, not when there is no baby in your uterus and that's all you dream of. It's actually very uncomfortable and filled me with sorrow.

Finally, I was called in to see the doctor and I told him about the pregnancy in July. Another scan, another blood test. I was also told that following the procedure, my uterus was completely fine, they'd not had to remove anything, it must just have been a shadow on that first scan. Essentially there was no reason they could see that I was miscarrying. Nothing in my blood, nothing physically. They told me to get back in contact when I was pregnant. When. I liked the use of the word when. Because I would be. Everyone said that was a good thing, that they didn't find any reason I'd lost my babies, but it didn't feel like it. With a reason, you can do something about it, no reason, well, there is no reason. So why? Why had not one of my babies lived? They were so much part of my life, all these investigations into their deaths had prolonged their active existence in my life and also reinforced their existence outside of just me, but, it meant the grief was also kept fresh.

Still, I had to keep moving forwards, I tried to avoid being emotional about any of this, for fear really that I was too broken, and the feelings would be insurmountable. Best to just plough on. Get back to being me. So now what? Decide when to do the IVF, decide whether to use a donor and decide when to stop and look at adoption. Onwards!

One of my close friends' daughter was 12 this year. When she was born, I thought my children would follow pretty quickly afterwards. I was once again struck with an awful feeling of loss. What have I done with my life? It's not like I built an amazing career instead, or went on amazing holidays, I've scrimped and saved to get a safe little home, to pay for IVF, to pay for dating websites and dinners, dating is really not cheap. I've tried to create the life I dreamt of. I have put so much effort into getting the family I want and look at where I am, no further ahead than in my 20's, except now I'm broken inside.

19th September 2016
My period started yesterday, and I couldn't face the day, I couldn't make myself get up, my chest hurt, from the massive lump in my throat all the way to below my heart. Like someone has my heart in a wrench, tightening its grip. My heart screams with his silent pain. Every month I convince myself I can feel something, twinges, headache. I'm sure this is it. How much more pain can my heart endure? I have waited so long for you my baby, where are you?

It's a harsh realisation that others have been pregnant as many times as me and now have that number of children, I still have none. I'm terrified that these will be my only experiences as a mother. One thing I have struggled with is that there is no evidence of my babies. If you have a stillbirth, you get a birth and death certificate, proof of your motherhood, proof of your baby. A legitimate loss. Mine all left too early to be acknowledged and that hurts massively. I bought myself a bracelet, with the birthstone, well death stone really, of when I'd lost each of my babies. I didn't know if that was a bit morbid, I felt silly, I'd not known these precious babies, but I had loved them and I wanted something to just be real and physical, to what was otherwise just my inner world. Having this bracelet really soothed me. I felt validated. I spent so much time in my head, it felt wonderful to have something I could touch which made it real.

I hate the fact that I feel like a lesser woman. I feel like I've not achieved anything, even though I have done ok in life. All that ever mattered to me was having a family of my own, so the rest just feels insignificant, empty. A hollow victory. I feel like I'm judged too, like I've just not tried hard enough, or must have done something wrong during the pregnancy, mustn't have taken enough care. Or, judged because I put my career first, waited too long. Whenever it comes up, I feel like shouting "I didn't choose to wait until now". I feel like I need to justify myself. I know I judge myself a lot too. I wonder why I care so much about how my life is perceived. I mean I know the truth, so does it matter? Thinking about it, I think it relates back to wanting to fit in. I always felt like I didn't really fit in, in so many ways. I felt that I was always, just between groups and that felt lonely.

That's what I feel now, I'm not part of the parent group, that's the gang I'm desperate to be in. I'm not in the don't want kids group, and I'm fighting tooth and nail to not be in the can't have kids group.

Being childless just isn't my future I was fighting this reality with every cell in my body. The universe seemed to think differently. The pain of being childless was unbearable. Just little every day things which made my life feel so insignificant. There are so many subliminal messages in society about what success looks like, throughout history and in every culture it has always been an important status symbol to have an heir, to bear children. To not have done so felt like such failure. I felt like a failure.

Sometimes I would think about the fact people could lose children through illness or accidents and wonder if I was better off having never had them to start with? I didn't have to face that worry. But then, most couples don't think of that before they have children, they just go ahead and deal with those situations when they occur, because having children is a natural part of continuation of the species. We are programmed to want this at a very basic biological level. I also don't think that anyone who ever lost a child regretted having them to start with. I didn't think I would. I didn't regret my pregnancies, in fact although they are forever tinged in sorrow, they were the happiest moments in my life. I loved being pregnant. I loved being mum to these tiny beings. I felt complete. For that short time, my soul did not feel like it was searching for something.

My soul. I talk about this a lot for someone who is not religious. I don't really even think of myself as spiritual, and yet I see magic in the beauty of nature. I feel calm in nature. In woods, by the sea, listening to birds in my garden. If I had to find spirituality it would be there, in my garden. A soul to me just means the core of your being, your personality. I also don't think souls are just for humans. I see a beautiful soul in my pets. I think, if I really think about it, its linked to affection and emotion, which you can see on a face, especially in the eyes.

Whatever a soul is, or mine is, I felt the same calmness and one-ness with life when I was pregnant as I do listening to early birdsongs with a cup of tea in my garden.

That Autumn, I started Level four of my Counselling and Psychotherapy qualification, the last two years before being qualified. As part of this course, I had to see a counsellor. You need to go through the process, for your own self development and increased self-awareness. You need to be able to separate what is your stuff and what is your clients', so you can keep the focus on your clients' agenda. The counsellor I had chosen this year seemed very kind. I walked into her front room and there was a picture of a brand-new baby. I felt the usual punch to the stomach. I sat and we talked. I felt instantly connected, we got on well and it was nice to be able to talk about the crazy going on inside, my anger, my hurt, my sorrow, that I tried so hard to hide from others, and partly from myself also. The following week, the picture had moved. I learnt later that this was her grandchild. She seemed barely older than me, that sense of panic about my age rumbled, ever present just under the surface.

I also had a placement working with Cruse Bereavement Care, a charity which provides support to those who are impacted by loss. I felt this was something I could empathise with easily, having been through several losses myself. I had done their training in the Spring and started seeing clients in the summer. I used to dread going to see clients, just because I dreaded having to be out there, with a sociable face on, but when I was with clients, who were in the throes of their grief, I felt that I could put mine aside. I was there to listen to theirs. They probably struggled to get out of their home to come and see me, just as much as I struggled and therefore, I felt connected to these people, who didn't know me, didn't know anything about me. My tutor always said that you get the clients you need, I know that sounds a little like destiny....but I do think it's true, that you are drawn to a specialism you can relate to and you get as much from spending time with clients as hopefully they get from time with you.

27th September 2016

Walking to the station this morning, as I got to the crossroads, I noticed a family also waiting to cross. A mother, with four children. I have a fleeting thought; how come she gets four? We could have shared out two each. That would have been fair.

Three; two; one

In October 2016 we started our IVF journey as a couple. It was lovely to walk into the clinic holding someone's hand. I was buzzing. This was it; this was going to be our chance for parenthood, I was for the first time in a long time filled with confidence and genuine excitement. We agreed to use my eggs during this first round, as if we could have afforded another round. Didn't matter, this would work.

IVF at Guys Hospital was such an amazing experience compared to Kings. The waiting room was smaller, felt less imposing. The consultant was kind. Once again however, we left the first appointment with bad news. I had a cyst on my ovary, and nothing further could be done until it had diminished. More waiting! I had to take the pill to try to reduce its size. I felt a pang of doubt, what if? What if this doesn't work? No time for that kind of thinking, of course it will work. It will work, this is our family.

Next time I went in, it had reduced, and we could go ahead. Guys was also very easy to get to from work, so far less awkward to find reasons for long absences during the day. Phew. I was only travelling up to Edinburgh once every 3 weeks now, so I was working from home a lot of the time, but I did go into the office in London Bridge to sit with some of my old colleagues at times. Work and fertility treatment are not a natural mix, unless you are completely open about it, which I have found it difficult to be. I felt guarded, because it was so important. First time because I was single and didn't want to be judged for making this choice alone. And also, for admitting failure in securing a relationship, something which I felt shame about and felt so alien, since all around me were couples. This time, I had so much riding on this, this felt like my last chance. I kept my cards very close to my chest.

I was so happy to have Paulo with me through all this, what a difference. My ovary once again was not very responsive, but I trusted this consultant, he seemed confident. He seemed to care about the outcome. Again, at the 11th hour my ovary rallied and eggs were produced. The eggs were harvested by general anaesthetic at this clinic. When I came out of the theatre, Paulo was waiting for me. Apparently, I was wheeled in singing the Cheeky Girls "touch my bum". I have no idea why, it's not a song I like or had heard recently. I wonder how I've behaved all the other times I've had a general anaesthetic. I've not had anyone in the room when I've come round before, I may have gone through a whole variety of one-hit wonders.

We got three eggs. Again, I heard the lady next to me being told they had got nine eggs from her. Three sounds such a tiny number. At least I could pull a face at Paulo this time. I remembered the words of that first embryologist, "it only takes one". All of them were fertilised and because of my age, all were put into my uterus. Three eggs. What if they all took? Triplets! I really hoped they would. One-stop family. That would be so amazing. I was so excited imagining telling people, not one, not two, but three babies. We had to wait the two weeks before we could test. It's a long two weeks.

Meanwhile, at work, I was coming to the end of my fixed term role and decided I was done trying to stay at that organisation so took the redundancy. I had been there a long time and therefore the package was pretty good. The next summer I was going to have qualified as a Counsellor and Psychotherapist. I had been wondering whether I could start my own practice as a Psychotherapist. Maybe with the redundancy money I could. It was scary, but I could maybe have a part time job with an agency and build up the practice slowly. My last day would be the 31st December, but since I'd accrued a lot of leave, I left in mid-December. It felt wonderful to have a break from the rat race. No commuting, nowhere I had to be, nothing I had to do. I was going to allow myself a month off before doing anything. Bliss.

I went to my mums that Christmas, with the amazing secret, I had three little eggs inside me. Paulo stayed with his family. Still, I felt amazing with my precious cargo. I talked to them. I actually felt pretty convinced that they would all stick. I remember seeing a picture of three little triplets and I saved it to my phone. I'd look at it every night before going to sleep and first thing in the morning, talking to my three eggs as I did. These could be mine. I'd have a whole family in one go. I didn't even worry about how I'd cope with three new-borns at once. I'd cope. People do.

Christmas day I woke up having had numerous dreams. I knew. I felt different. This was the most perfect present in the world. When I got back from my mums, I took the test. Pregnant. I knew it! This was perfect. We were both so excited, but also quite cautious. It's difficult to invest so much in something and have to hold back from any excitement. I know that I struggled to not plan ahead. Plan our family, all five of us. Just normal daily life, maybe doing some baking. Playing in the garden. I could picture them, in the world where I truly belonged. I could almost hear their giggles and little feet running around. I tried so hard to not let my mind get carried away. I told my close friends that I was pregnant.

Two weeks later I went to the Recurrent Miscarriage Clinic, where I had a scan and more blood tests. The scan showed two healthy sized little embryos and two little heartbeats. Twins. Two little miracle babies. I cried. I could not stop the tears. The consultant was very sweet, handed me a box of tissues. I asked about taking Aspirin. He didn't think I needed it; he said my blood did not show any evidence that it was necessary. My blood didn't show any reason that I would miscarry. However, I had read a lot of scientific evidence that a small dose of Aspirin helped, and some IVF clinics actually prescribed it as part of the treatment. I knew that you shouldn't start it too early or it could increase the chances of miscarriage. I also knew you shouldn't continue it too late into the pregnancy. I remembered the words of the A&E doctor a couple of years ago and decided I would take a mini aspirin. I started with half of a mini aspirin every other day; I felt a bit guilty taking it when the consultant had said it wasn't necessary.

I didn't tell anyone we were having twins. I thought that would be such a lovely surprise. I imagined all the super happy faces when we'd walk in, each of us cradling one baby. It never really occurred to me to worry about the twins. This was destiny (I know, I don't believe in it). All the pain I'd been through was to get me to this point, to these twins which were my family. I loved being pregnant again. I felt so sick, it was glorious. I was exhausted. I had so many headaches, was hot and sweaty at night, couldn't sleep well, couldn't sleep on my front, which is my normal sleeping position. It was all wonderful. The long wait was over, this was it. My joy could not be restrained, I felt like I was walking on air. I was thinking which twin pram we would have, side by side or one in front of the other? Which works better on public transport or in shops?

But how would the twins feel if they weren't able to sit next to one another? I was so excited for my belly to show, it would show sooner, with two. Also, I had read that it shows earlier in second pregnancies, or fifth in my case. Would my previous one's count, since they ended so early? I doubted it, but hoped all the same.

A couple of weeks later, I went to Guys to have a scan with them. They could only see one heartbeat. I told them the Recurrent Miscarriage Clinic in Paddington had found two, they searched for it, but there was definitely only one heartbeat. I was crushed.

My heart hurt. I had hoped for three, but was overjoyed with two, now we were down to one precious baby. Part of me hoped that it was just that maybe one was in front of the other or something, maybe there were still two? It's so hard to accept your baby is gone. My hope was unstoppable sometimes, but mostly I believed there was just one now. I was so torn, trying to stay happy and positive to ensure only positive vibes and hormones are reaching the remaining baby, whilst still being heartbroken at losing yet another baby.

It was hard, because nobody knew I was pregnant with twins, so how could I tell them I had lost a baby? I was still pregnant, so as far as they knew, nothing had changed. I wished I'd not been so foolish as to imagine the fun surprise of twins. My stupid confidence that this was it, this was my family. I tried to explain my heartache to my close friends, without saying there had been twins, I didn't want them to feel I'd lied to them and now, why tell them about a baby which was no longer there? I said they had concerns at the clinic but didn't say I'd lost a baby.

I made the usual calls, to the midwife, to the Early Pregnancy Unit. A dating appointment was booked. The Early pregnancy unit with its many pregnant women. I had to keep reminding myself I was one of them. I was rightfully there. The further scan here confirmed this. I was relieved. This baby was fine.

Sometime later I realised I didn't feel so sick anymore. That feeling of dread overwhelmed me. I'd ask Paulo if I was still pregnant, he'd tell me not to worry. I think he thought I just worried too much because of what we'd been through. The next day I'd feel really sick again, which would reassure me. This carried on for a while. I met the midwife, it was so difficult when she asked if I had any previous pregnancies, to recount them all, re-live them. I then had to go back to the Recurrent Miscarriage Clinic for another scan. I went into the room, got on the bed and had the freezing gel put onto my stomach. The scanner was placed on my tummy, it was moved around, it was pressed down harder. A wave of panic hit me. The lady left the room saying she would be back shortly and came back in followed by a gentleman who took the scanner. The same searching, pressing uncomfortably.

No, there was no heartbeat.

10th February 2017

This morning I was told there was no heartbeat. I have lost two more babies. Six in total now. Six babies that weren't you. I cannot believe I have to go through this again. The pain.

My babies.

My turn.

I cannot bear this.

How do I get through this?

Two days later, I had the miscarriage. I don't remember this miscarriage at all. I know it was painful, because I was told. I know Paulo went to stock up on a huge amount of pain relief drugs and sanitary products. I know I felt as if the whole of me fell out, my entire body, my soul, my hope, my heart. I don't remember if it was night or day or how long it took. I don't remember being on the loo. I don't remember being at all. I didn't write in my diary. I wasn't working, which made it easier, in that I didn't have to pretend. I didn't have to get up or think about anything. However, I don't really remember much, I think I've blocked this one out entirely. The week after, I had to go back to the Early Pregnancy Unit, with all its pregnant women full of hope, to hear once again what I knew, that I had officially lost the babies. I could not get my head around it.

I had to go back to the Recurrent Miscarriage Clinic the following week, so they too, could confirm I'd lost my babies. I remember being sat near the passage with my back to the other clinic. I heard a happy little gurgle and looked round to see a baby, about one year old, stood just looking at me. She had curly blonde hair and blue eyes, she had slightly rosy, chubby cheeks and a beautiful smile. Just how I imagined my children would look. She reached her hand out and held the armrest of my chair. My heart felt like it was in a vice. I felt like time had gone into slow motion as I watched her. I wanted to scoop her up. I wanted her to be mine. I also wanted to jump out of my chair and scream "get away from me!". She was so scrumptious, and I couldn't stand to have her near me, like she was radioactive. What was wrong with me? My heart's silent scream of pain shot out of me, like a searchlight. I could feel again. I cried. I cried all through my consultation with the doctor, I cried the whole journey home, I cried when I got home. I cried for days.

Paulo and I went back to Guys to discuss how we moved forward. The consultant was sorry for our loss but said that I was likely to just continue miscarrying. Seems we don't move forward. We talked about donor eggs, but he said that I would miscarry again. It felt like the land before me had opened up, I could see into the darkness below. How do you stop yourself falling?

Later I thought about what he had said and I felt that he did not think there was anything wrong with my eggs. I mean I guess he had seen the three eggs which were fertilised and placed back inside. I am sure he would not be able to know that early, that there were no chromosomal issues with them, but I hoped that maybe with years of experience he could hazard a guess? Who knows, but he seemed to think I was miscarrying, rather than they weren't developing correctly. In a very strange way, I find that comforting. They were ok, they were growing fine. My beautiful babies. I was the one who did it wrong. My darling little babies were amazing.

I had wanted those twins so, so badly. I had believed this was it, I had never even thought to doubt this pregnancy. I'd been so confident. I loved them so much. I had believed they were my family. I was so sure this time. I was so heartbroken, mixed in with fury. That the clinic would let me pay for something which would fail. Furious no one had found a reason. Furious that I hadn't been told to take aspirin, maybe if I'd not been scared to take it in earnest, this could have been avoided? Furious that I'd not been given any immuno-suppressants. I felt taking them, even if unnecessary would have been better than doing nothing. Considering nothing else has come up, surely by process of elimination, I am just attacking my own babies? From the research I have done, this does appear to be a very feasible reason. How had the recurrent miscarriage clinic not seen this? They had tested everything. Could this be such a subtle change that it wouldn't show up in a blood test? I had trusted them.

I had to tell people again that I'd lost my babies. I had to say that I'd lost two. I felt guilty for having lied about the twins. It wasn't a lie; I was hoping to have such a happy surprise for everyone who had been so supportive throughout my journey. I felt shame that I had to admit my failure again. Failure as a woman, failure as a mum. Failure to fit in. I had run out of strength to do this.

I was glad it was half-term. In January, I had started working as a School Counsellor with Place2Be, a charity which works within schools, with any children who require some additional support, as part of my Counselling and Psychotherapy qualification. I was seeing three young clients every week. I was not at the school the following week, but the week after I was back. It was so hard, I'd go in, as all the kids were arriving. It being primary school, many of them had younger siblings who would drop them off too. I was surrounded by babies. I had so dreamed it would be my turn to do the school run soon. I would walk into school holding back tears. I'd go and hide in the counselling room and pull myself together. I loved my time with the children I saw, but it was an excruciating time also.

13th March 2017

I just don't know how to be ok about this. Six babies just gone. My beautiful little twins gone? It's not ok! My heart feels ripped out of my body. My future vanished in a puff of smoke.

This diary has been going for 10 years and I'm still childless. This started off to help my adopted or sperm-donor baby understand my decision, now it's just a tale of loss and love I have for every single baby I've held in my womb. I love you my babies. I miss who we'd have been. I wish you could have stayed with me.

I feel like a rabbit in headlights, I can't see, I don't know which direction to take. Nowhere feels safe. I've lost me.

I knew that I couldn't start up my own practice now, you have to invest so much of yourself when setting up alone. I could barely cope with getting out of bed. Most days I just sat and stared. I'd put the telly on, but I didn't know what was on, I don't remember seeing anything. One of my first jobs after university was working in pensions and I'd learnt that you should always sign on if not at work, since this counts towards your pensionable years. I went to sign on.

The lady I spoke to didn't even understand what a Change Manager was, she'd have definitely not been able to help. I think she'd have been happy for me to just get a job anywhere doing anything, not actually follow a career. I wanted a job, for the financial security, but I also wanted it to be the right one. She wanted me to apply for anything, I was being picky. The trouble was, I couldn't tear myself out of the bottom of my bed in the mornings, let alone give two hoots about finding a job. I couldn't bring myself to care. I felt like the first time I went to the Planetarium when I was eight years old and realised how small and insignificant our lives are in the universe. Everything felt meaningless.

Mother's Day loomed once again. I sent a card to my mum. I felt such dread for the day. Another time of year when I try to avoid contacting my friends with young children, I avoid social media, I avoid shops. I don't want to see the hand-made card, or love heart or flowers picked by just the head, like only young children do. It wasn't just that I wasn't a mum, I felt that I was a mum, just not officially, not worthy of a card, because my babies hadn't lived. I felt again like I lived in some kind of parallel world. I thought of the quantum physics theory that for every event which happens, there's a parallel universe where this event did not happen. That means that somewhere out there, there's a universe where my babies all lived. Or maybe one or two of them lived. I like this idea.

One of my friends sent me such a beautiful gift, a silver necklace with a little baby feet pendant, and around it was written 'always in my heart'. I felt amazing wearing this, it was like I was wearing my babies next to my heart. I wish they really were. I saw a miscarriage quote, about how your baby knows how much you loved them, because they are the only ones who know what your heart sounds like on the inside. I miss my babies so much. Every day. I don't want this reality.

I remember searching wildly for support, for someone who would understand, for answers. I trawled the web. I found a charity called Aching Arms. That's how mine felt, empty, but oh so achy. I was supposed to have one baby in each arm, I longed to feel the ache because of the weight of my children, the empty ache was far heavier to bear. This charity gives teddy bears to women who have lost a baby, something to hold in memory of your baby. The kind lady I spoke to asked if I wanted a bear sent to me. I remembered little patch, the dog my mum had given me. I still couldn't look at him, he was still at the back of the drawer I'd hidden him in almost two years ago now. A bear would not make this better. I declined but felt that it was a really lovely idea. Maybe when I feel a bit better about this. But surely, I needed six bears?

In April, an agency contacted me about a job as a Change Manager for a large organisation. I had an interview and got it, and then had to wait several weeks to pass the security clearance required to work in this organisation. I think the delayed start was a good thing, allowing me time to grieve and be in a better place to cope with work. I think I needed that time. I would be based in Westminster, which was a nice commute from home, 25 minutes train journey and then a walk up from Charring Cross Station.

Unfortunately, I joined a team where one lady was four months pregnant. I remember one of my first few days there, she started talking to me about having started wearing pregnancy tights and how amazing they were. I just sat there thinking 'seriously?' I know this was her first pregnancy and she was excited about her belly growing. That's normal. Losing six babies isn't normal. There is no reason she would assume that I was consumed with grief. I'm not sure how managed to act as if everything was fine, maybe I hadn't, maybe she thought I was completely disinterested in babies? I wasn't even concerned what she thought of me, I was still very numb. I was just trying to make it through the day, however I could. I did not have enough left-over energy to care about someone else. Seems motherhood was still chasing me, still haunting me.

I went to my mum's for her birthday in May. The flight back, I was sat the seat in front of a mum and a very, very young baby. He cried. I felt like a caged tiger. I wanted to get away, to get so far away from the cry, not because it was annoying or loud, but because it ripped through my soul. I turned my music on as loud as I could bear. It couldn't drown him out. I felt like my skin was on fire, such was the desire to get away from this torture. My uterus had by now tied itself into all sorts of knots.

The food trolley came out. I turned towards the window and closed my eyes so that no one would notice how red and puffy they were by now. The tears just kept coming, a continuous flow. I felt sick, I felt trapped inside my skin. I couldn't get away. I willed the flight to hurry. At last the baby stopped crying. The flight is only just over an hour, we were almost there now. It took me a couple of hours to get home from the airport and my eyes were still red and puffy when I got home, I must have looked a right mess getting off that flight. It's a wonder Border control could recognise me from my passport picture. Much greater than my fear of flying, this one flight has made me dread flying.

College was tough, trying to be ok when I was so broken. I think there were glimpses, my tutor was aware of how broken I was, but I think few others were. I kept things on quite a superficial level in terms of what I disclosed, whilst not lying. I never made out I was happy. They knew I had previously miscarried, but this one was too raw to talk about yet, although I did in my journals, which is why my tutor knew. That year, two of my college friends had been pregnant. I had found it so difficult, as their bellies grew, as they discussed the pregnancies and any concerns or hopes. They were both friends and yet I really struggled to sit with them. I couldn't look at the bump. Sometimes I would make myself do it, because I cared for these friends, I felt I had to put my internal world, my insular hurt aside. I needed to be present in this world, the real world. But I could feel the baby again, like a magnet, pulling on my uterus. I could feel my uterus like when I had been pregnant. I wanted to cradle my own stomach. I had so loved being pregnant, feeling the little life of my child within me. It was unbearable pain, which to this day I've not told them. It's such an awful thing to admit to, feeling so much pain, over something so joyous.

Groundhog Life

My heart breaks a million times each day
I feel the void, the emptiness
Why couldn't you stay?
I see mothers with their babies,
How did they get to hold theirs?
My eyes fill
I try to blink the tears away
But the pain in my soul takes over
My eyes burn, tears fall, I feel shame
My broken heart, I could not contain

I imagine you all now
What you'd be doing
Who you would be
How I would feel holding your tiny hand
Life continues around me
Ordinary daily concerns
While I am crushed on the floor
Trying so hard to scrape myself off it
Trying to care, trying to smile
Zombie days

Someone asks how I am
I reply "fine", with a smile
Where did I find the strength for that?
We talk, I act normal
Like nothing is missing, like I am whole
My heart screams "my babies died"
You were so real to me
So easy to forget in this nightmare state
I miss the me I should be
I miss you

A baby cries, a baby giggles
My uterus feels hollow, empty, burgled
My legs at the ready, I have to escape
I feel so trapped
My heart aches like a gaping wound
I turn my music up
It drowns nothing out
I am filled with pain; I am nothing else
Anger consumes, why me, why mine?
Life haunts me

Then at last daylight

Hope, joy, I am back
But someone mentions a birthday
An event, just a day
Families in adverts and programmes
Someone gets pregnant,
congratulations, yay
Constant reminders that you are not
here
Every day normality taunts me
My love is trapped in a broken heart
Too many tiny pieces to put back
together

Another day, the sun shines
For a second, life is fine
Then I remember I carried you
And you all left me, my love had
nowhere to go
My body feels heavy
I'm supposed to be better
My whole future has evaporated
What if this is it?
What if you were my only chances?
I don't know how to be ok that you
died?

Woke up again, endless days without you
All I can feel is my aching heart
My shattered dreams
I've waited forever for you
I loved you
You were supposed to arrive
My life would start
Takes everything I have just to get out of bed
To put on my public face
Groundhog life

May 2017

Driving home for Christmas

Being at work again was tough. Most days I was having to scrape myself up, off the floor. I'd put on my work clothes, hoping they could somehow hold me together, contain my grief, give me a human shape, provide me with the strength to stand which my bones seem to lack. I was so lost, I felt so much sorrow and anger. My babies just vanished. How was I supposed to look at the world now? I felt I had been robbed, violated. My babies, my life, stolen. The world felt like such a hostile place.

The world, all sunny and spring-like, acting like life is the priority, flowers blooming, the trees finding their leaves, everything looked normal on the outside, when in fact it was stealing away babies. My babies.

29 June 2017

I can't bear it, my heart aches so much. I hate the fact that I'm powerless. I hate that.

I can't bear the pain. I want to just be at home, under my duvet, crying. I don't want to put on a brave face today. It's too hard. I don't want to stop myself crying. I don't want to see people and smile. I want to allow my emotions, I want to feel fully sad, allow that sadness, miss you properly.

The physical pain of the miscarriages has I think traumatised me somewhat. I have never felt pain like it. It's as if your soul is separating from your body. The pain is so excruciating. The desire to stop it happening so strong. The powerlessness so overwhelming. I feel like I was physically torn apart.

I'm sorry. I'm so sorry I got it wrong. Sorry I let you down. This wasn't supposed to be how your life went. Sorry I couldn't hold on to you. Sorry I couldn't stop you leaving. I tried so hard to keep you.

I was so relieved when my placement at Place2Be broke up for the summer, although I had still managed to enjoy my sessions with the children, it had been so hard to walk in during the school run. At least at the end of the day, I would have supervision, so thankfully all the children and parents had gone by the time I was walking out.

Over the last few years, I have lost connections with friends, either because they were uncomfortable with my losses, or because I have withdrawn. I found many situations too painful. I found it difficult to ask friends who were pregnant or had new babies how they were. I so wanted to be pregnant, I so wanted to have had my own baby. I couldn't bear hearing about feeling tired because your baby kept you up. I hadn't slept in months due to my grief.

I became quite addicted to Pinterest; I'd look at mindless pictures late into the night to avoid my thoughts. I would love there to be a baby keeping me awake instead of my broken mind and shattered heart. I wouldn't visit people with young babies for self-preservation. I have a wide variety of age-groups in my friendship circles, from school, university, various jobs, charity placements and evening college. I've watched people of my age go on to have their families but then also those 5, 10 and now 15 years younger than me. Obviously, its life, that's what happens to most people. I'm now in the >1% of women who have more than three miscarriages.

I also lost a connection to a lot of the cultural festivities which formed part of who I was. Christmas was always my favourite day, but I find this time of year unbearable now. It's meant to be with families, it's meant to have children. Easter was always a big family time with us, as was the Swiss National day. I always just wanted a family with my parents around to know my children, babysit, or just spend the day with us. To watch my parents be grandparents would make me feel I had fulfilled my role in the great circle of life.

My grief seemed to know no end after losing the twins. The loss felt compounded. I hadn't just lost the twins, I felt like I had lost each of my babies I'd lost before at the same time. Each miscarriage is also the loss of opportunity, each pregnancy could very easily be my last, so I don't just lose that one, or two babies but the opportunity of ever having a baby of my own. I think grief, certainly for me is linked not only to the love you have for the person, but also the loss of future and potential, which would explain the huge depth of the loss I felt for the babies I'd never even met. There was so much left unfinished, unlived. I just wished it wasn't real.

I know that I judged myself harshly, wanting a magic formula to finish this endless pain that I couldn't drag myself out of. I felt guilty for not being involved in friends' lives, for withdrawing, for finding situations too difficult or triggering. I felt I should know better, logically I knew that my feelings were just that, fleeting emotions given power by my thoughts. Now I look back with more kindness on the me back then. I was hurt, beyond words. I found life hard. I was doing my best to just make it through and protecting myself as I could. Grief is hard. Like such a huge weight. I physically felt I was dragging that weight around with me.

As I came to the end of the first year of Counselling and Psychotherapy Level four, I decided I would take a break from seeing my counsellor too. We had done some really useful work over the last few months, I had processed a lot, but it was time. It was also expensive, but I felt we'd got to a point now where she no longer held the boundaries, I felt she was trying to 'heal' me, to find a solution. She bought up adoption more and more, I was still unwilling to accept that I would not get pregnant. I would not entertain the thought of becoming comfortable with not carrying my own child.

In hindsight I'd not really let it sink in that I would always miscarry my pregnancies. Motherhood was so much part of my identity; I didn't know how not to be that person. I was unwilling to accept that I would not 'finish' pregnancy. Now I think part of my unwillingness to let go is just the grief of loss. When you lose someone, you want them back. I wanted my babies back; I wanted my pregnancy back. I wanted my motherhood. I think deep down if someone had given me a baby and said it was mine to keep, my desire for pregnancy above anything else would have waned. I love babies, but they don't have to be mine biologically. I think adoption felt difficult to accept because there is always a link to the birth mother, and I felt this would somehow lessen my motherhood.

However, we did talk about adoption and what I would do with my counsellor. I spoke about going back to work, hopefully with less hours. My counsellor then said, "so you would adopt this child and then let someone else look after it?" Again with the benefit of hindsight, I don't think she meant anything by that, she potentially was meaning after all the pain of waiting for my motherhood to start, but at the time I felt judged. I had to pay bills. I didn't have the luxury of being able to not work.

19th July 2017

Sometimes I feel that the only thing holding me together is the air around me. I feel so fragile, if I don't hold on incredibly tightly then I'd fall into a tiny patch of dust.

Time passed. Time. Something I have such a fraught relationship with. I wanted to speed it up to a moment when I felt my life could start but was conscious that too much time had already passed, I needed to slow it down, turn it back. I was old in the fertility world. I felt so broken, everything felt wrong, everything felt like a contradiction. I still loved my children, my children which seemed to just refuse to exist, to manifest themselves into real life.

Year two of Counselling and Psychotherapy Level four started in the Autumn and with it, I started seeing a new counsellor. My tutor had challenged me to find someone that I'd not usually have gone with. There's usually a lot which can be learnt from challenging yourself in that way. So, I decided it had to be a man, since I felt they would never understand my deep-seated desire for motherhood. I found a gentleman who was local. He did walking therapy. I was intrigued. I have always felt better when I was in nature, even just gardening I find it to be a very mindful experience, when I feel my hurt actually subsides. I thought this could be brilliant. He had some time available and recommended 8am on a Saturday morning. I am not a morning person. His reasoning was sound, it was quieter in the parks at that time, but first thing in the morning, my brain speeds are similar to when I'm drunk. We compromised on 8.30. I went along with a little trepidation. I talked, he listened. I never felt judged. So began our work together.

In October, feeling that we really needed to move things along, with Paulo's agreement, I contacted a local Council with regards to adoption and a very kind lady came round to talk to us about it. I had read about the foster-to-adopt and was keen on this option. She spoke about adoption in general, things to consider, such as not using the Council nearest where you live, because of the chances of meeting family members, in shops or at a local school etc. She also told us about another Council having the most foster-to-adopt cases and therefore being a good option. Far enough away to not bump into families, but close enough to enable regular meetings with the social workers. She also said that out of 19 foster-to-adopt babies, 18 went on to be adopted by the foster parents. These were good odds. But, what if we were that 19th couple? Could I cope with losing another baby? Statistics have not been on my side on this quest to motherhood.

11th November 2017

I still can't believe you're not here. I have loved you for so long. I have waited to meet you for so long. I've not been myself in so long. I feel like I'm living a half-life, half alive, half not. You learn to look and behave like a normal 3D person, when actually, you feel hollow inside. Everything hurts.

Every day I walk into work, dreading a day of smiling and being friendly. Fighting tears. On my return to the station in the evening I lose the fight, it's so exhausting to keep up the false self, the tears just roll down my cheeks on my walk. Then back to being 'normal' when I get to the station. No one can see the real me.

Tonight, I went out with some of the old crew. I love them, it's always a fun night, but I feel like a fraud, being half there. Tonight, someone mentioned something, about 'when' they have kids, just that confident assumption that of course they will, because that's what happens. I realise I don't belong with these people. Where what is meant to happen does happen. I don't live in their world. We share space, but I don't fit in.

I hope no one noticed the cold wave of despair which washed over me, the sinking pain, like being forced to swallow a solid piece of ice-cold rock. I managed to hold on until the walk home from the station. The tears flowed, streaming down my face, warm against my cold face. I came in and Matilda came to greet me at the door. I fell to my knees and sobbed on my hall floor. I had no strength left.

I miss you, I wanted you so much. I miss me. I don't know if I'll ever feel like me again. Joy and hope seem so alien.

I felt so stupid to have assumed it would happen. I still had the pregnancy books in my Amazon basket from my first pregnancy with Paulo, there was a book in there for him too. I was just waiting until we'd got beyond the three months to order it. I found it unbearable to see it, but also could not bring myself to remove it from my basket, that was admitting defeat. That little spark of hope just wouldn't allow me to. That spark, just making me believe in what could never be. I almost felt mistrust for hope. Look where it's got me, more pain. And yet I needed to find joy again somehow, I needed to fill the hole where my heart and soul once lived.

I had been thinking about getting a dog for a while. I always wanted a dog, long before I thought about getting a cat. Back when I was a young child, I would write puppy on my Christmas list every year. For the last year or so, I had been doing research on dog breeds. I needed a dog that was good with cats and good with children. We'd even gone to the Pet Show at Olympia back in May, so I could talk to breeders. So many of them had cats as well as dogs. I had always dreamt of having a Border Collie, but I had to be realistic, we lived in London, with just a standard garden and both worked full time. Also, I know that on a dark, wet, cold winter's day, I will not want to go out for a couple of hours walk after work. I needed to be fair to the dog, so I started looking at 'apartment friendly' breeds. I was also looking up various dog types on Pinterest and had fallen in love with one in particular. A Cavapoo. This dog was beautiful. This was the dog I wanted.

I would have liked a rescue dog, but neither of us have had dogs before and I was always a bit scared of dogs as a child. I wanted to know this dog from the start, know what they had been through, so I could trust this dog with my cat and later my children. I had read that cats already established in a household take to puppies much better than older dogs, since they sense these are babies and therefore not a threat. I also wanted a baby. Albeit a fur-baby. I had made contact in December with an organisation who rehomed but also bred Cavapoos. I asked if I could be added to their waiting list. The next available puppies would be in April. I felt a huge wave of relief, a baby I could love, a baby I could actually keep! Only a few short months.

My placement at Place2Be ended at Christmas. I had enjoyed it and had initially hoped I could keep going until the next summer, but I was finding the condensed weeks really difficult, since work was incredibly busy. I was working much longer days anyway just because of workload, let alone making up for an additional day. I was saddened to leave my young clients, they had been amazing, I had loved working with them. However, I was not going to miss the school run, all the babies and smug mums whom I felt, just looked through you if you weren't walking with a child. I felt shunned by this gang I'd failed to become a member of.

As Christmas loomed, my period was due. I had felt some twinges and felt hot at night. I remember talking to my counsellor about the fact my body had been playing tricks on me over the last couple of years, giving me symptoms of early pregnancy just before my period started and how it was just another heart-breaking reminder of what I didn't have, probably couldn't have.

A few days later, when it still hadn't arrived, I took a test. I was pregnant. I almost couldn't believe it. We were still trying but not as enthusiastically as previously. I was a mum for Christmas, albeit just a pregnant one. I tried not to think that this was the third time I'd been pregnant over Christmas and was still facing it childless. We drove over to my mums this year together, having agreed the previous year that we'd never be apart again over Christmas. I was overjoyed with our little secret. I remember being in the car, our first family road trip. I felt whole. I felt alive. Add a decent dollop of Christmas magic, this was the one.

Now I wonder how I managed to believe each time, but when you are in the middle of a situation, you don't necessarily realise the repetition in what you are living. Now, looking back I wonder how I managed to feel this excited, with everything I'd been through. I always felt so right being pregnant that I couldn't not believe in it. I felt all the hope I thought I'd lost forever come crashing back into my life. It was like it had all been held back by some sort of dam and the dam had been broken. I was overwhelmed with excitement for the future. I could breathe again.

I waited several weeks before contacting the Recurrent Miscarriage Clinic, I wanted to relish the joy of being pregnant. In the end I went, I had a scan and they took blood, they confirmed the pregnancy, there was a heartbeat, it was real. I had got to a point of not trusting myself or my body on this. So, feeling more confident, I contacted the normal Midwife and Early Pregnancy Unit. I went in for a first scan there, excited. They asked why I'd waited so long to go and see them, I felt reprimanded. I replied that I didn't have any positive experiences in the EPU, and I had put it off, it's really not somewhere I've longed to get back to, too many awful memories. The cold gel, a moment of dread, I held my breath. Please be ok, please still be there. That look, the quiet. The scanner being moved, slowly at first and then more urgently. I knew. I felt myself falling. I barely heard the "I'm sorry, there is no heartbeat". My ears felt like they froze over at the sound, the freeze travelling over my whole body.

Those words again. Words that just break your very soul. The familiar silent scream of anguish starting up in my heart, my heart that I felt sure was by now just a series of thousands of small pieces residing in the same vicinity. There's not a chance it was still solid, still intact. Sometimes I wonder if its scream of pain really is silent, or if I'm so distanced from reality in that moment that it's an audible one?

I had to go in to see the doctor. They took me straight through, from the scan, no waiting in with the other pregnant ladies this time. I wished they had done that the other times I'd been. The doctor offered me some medication to bring on the miscarriage. This is the first time I'd been offered this. All the previous times, I'd seen a female doctor. All the previous times they'd told me my baby was dead and made me sit with the pregnant ladies again until I was called in to see the doctor. This was the first male doctor and he offered me something to make it a less traumatic experience. I suspected the female doctors had never experienced a miscarriage for themselves. But nor would he. Odd that he was showing more empathy.

I didn't know whether I wanted to or not. When you're pregnant and you are told your baby has died, you can't believe it, or certainly I can't. It's my baby, my very life. I'm still alive, so how can my baby not be? It's impossible to get your head around. So, to take something which would bring on the loss of it felt very wrong. This must just be a mistake. However, I knew deep down it wasn't. I took the drugs and it happened fairly quickly and far less painfully than all but one of the others. I wonder what my experience of miscarriage would be if they had all been like this? Maybe I wouldn't have felt so traumatised? I wouldn't have had the awful flashbacks of begging my child to stay. Of dreading going to the toilet. Of reliving it every time I go to the toilet. The agonising hours on the loo, the blood, the pain, pins and needles in your legs but unable to step away for more than a couple of minutes as the flow just keeps coming. Why was this the first time I had been offered these drugs?

Once again, I did not write the next entry in my diary to my child.

24th January 2018

This is so ridiculous; I could almost laugh. I was just over nine weeks pregnant and I miscarried my seventh baby on Saturday. Since then I have felt numb. I don't feel like I'm grieving. I just feel like there's no me left. I can't concentrate on anything, I don't care. I'm just an empty shell. Vacant.

I called work and said I had flu. I had a couple of days of just doing nothing and then worked from home. I think what was different this time is that I felt I couldn't do this again. It felt very final. I felt that hope was now well and truly gone. I was coming up to my 42nd birthday, I was really struggling to get pregnant. The miscarriage risk goes up every time you have a miscarriage, not to mention the risk at my age, which also jumps up hugely.

I dreaded telling people, again. Surely, I've drained all the sympathy anyone can offer one person in a lifetime? I don't want to be Mrs Bad-News and yet it feels that's all I ever have to share with anyone. I never get to give the good life announcements, engagement, pregnancy (I never made an official announcement, just told close friends), our baby girl or boy has been born, I don't get to share happy photos of my kids, proud dad, family days out, first day of school, with friends, with my mum. No, just Mrs Bad-News over here. I can't bring myself to tell anyone. But I have to. I can't just stay quiet, I'd told close friends I was pregnant again, they'd notice if in a few months that there is no baby. That's the crux of it. There is no baby. I'm empty. Again. I found a picture recently, a pencil drawing of a pregnant woman, where the stomach has been rubbed out, but you can just see the faint traces of a pregnant belly, underneath it says, 'erased'. That's how I feel. My baby was stolen away from me.

I had told my counsellor before Christmas that I was fed up with my body playing tricks on me and giving me pregnancy symptoms just before my period started, little did I know that at that time, it was finally not a hoax, it was real. I hadn't told him I was pregnant, I'm not sure why not, since I talked about a lot of very personal feelings with him. Now I had to see him again and explain that I had been pregnant, but I had now lost another baby. I really felt his sadness for me.

One of my close friends had lost her first baby in November, I was so gutted for her, I know that this had been quite a journey for her too. We met shortly after I'd had my miscarriage. It was lovely to see her, but such a sad encounter, we were both hurt. I wanted to support her, she had lost her first baby, that's a shocker to any new mum, but I felt so incredibly broken and ended up crying myself. Shortly after, she sent me an article, about how it's been found that a small part of every baby, including those miscarried remain in a woman's body. I loved this article. A small part of my babies was still here, within me. They had existed. They were real.

29th January 2018

I feel like I'm at a crossroads and all the signs are in a foreign language. Which direction do I chose? How do I know?

The social

I needed to accept carrying my own baby was unlikely now. I was too old to keep trying and losing babies, especially with the fact I was struggling to get pregnant at all. I read an article which stated after the age of 45 there is close to zero chance you will get pregnant naturally, that age was looming ever closer. The words of the Guys consultant, that I would always miscarry my pregnancies rang loud and clear around my head. He had been proved right after the last pregnancy. I felt I was flogging a dead horse and was exhausted by it.

It's a truth I struggled to accept. I had done so much to avoid this. It made therapy difficult. Acceptance is a huge part of healing and I had been refusing to. It also made moving forwards with other solutions difficult and led to procrastination. I'd watched too much Disney in my time, I just assumed that in the end, everything would work out ok, the ending is always happy.

My counsellor was a huge help. I have never felt less judged nor more listened to as with him. I was wrong to assume you needed to have felt your uterus do a back-flip when you hear a baby cry to understand the pain I felt. He let me feel my pain, didn't try to cheer me up, or tell me how grateful I should be about having this or that. He didn't mention any 'at least's', diminishing my loss. He just walked with me and accepted my pain and in doing so I felt entirely understood. I owe so much to this man who slowly helped me to breathe again.

I had so much built up love for all the babies I'd had and lost, I could feel it almost physically, like I may burst. Love doesn't go anywhere when someone dies, it lingers, with nowhere to go. I think this is what the pain of grief is, the love that has lost its rightful home. I contacted the lady I'd spoken to about a Cavapoo puppy. She told me she had forgotten to put me on their waiting list for April and that the next opportunity would be October. I couldn't wait any longer to plough my love into a baby, any baby. I was ridiculously devastated.

I had a few days over at my mums. I was filled with the usual sense of failure. I didn't tell her about this loss. I think I was quite vacant and numb whilst there. Luckily my mum slept most of the day and since she was moving into sheltered housing, I concentrated on packing boxes. It was mindless and could be done easily enough in a blur of numbness.

Paulo could see that I was really struggling and whilst I was away, he looked locally for any Cavapoo puppies and found some close by. There was one still available. The guy wanted to meet us first and a deposit to save the puppy. The evening I flew back we went to see the puppy. I don't think once you've seen a puppy you can walk away from it. They were good to go to their new homes the following day and he said we could even take her that evening, I so wanted to, but it was late evening and we had nothing ready.

The next day we got up early, went to Pets at Home and bought everything we thought we'd need, and a lot more besides. Then, with our little blanket ready to get the scent of the mum, we went to pick up our puppy, Chloe. I sat in the car, holding this precious baby as if she was made of glass and I cried. I was bringing a baby home. A living, breathing, heart-beating baby to love.

I was terrified that something would happen to my little puppy. My track record with babies being as it was, I was almost scared to love her too much. I didn't trust that she'd stay in my life long. She was impossible to resist however and gave me a joyful reason to get up every day. We knew nothing about dogs but had read that crate training was the way forwards. She'd wake us in the (very early) morning, hopping from leg to leg, sometimes jumping with both legs, making the cutest little "Boop, boop, boop" noise. She would be there waiting for me; her tail would be wiggling her entire body along with it. I'd get her out and we'd snooze for another hour or so together on the sofa, until it was time to get ready for work. I hated leaving her, but we had a lovely dog-walker who came to puppy sit twice a day when I went into the office. Slowly, Chloe bought me back to life.

27th February 2018

I don't remember much of the last month. For a time, I felt I hadn't been affected half as much as losing the twins last year. I mean last year I could barely stand up; I couldn't spend an hour without sobbing. I didn't have any of that this year. I almost seemed to cope fine. And yet in hindsight now, I still had the shock, I still had the numbness, I don't really remember much at all.

I think what makes this time worse is that I feel I'm not grieving the loss of my baby so much as I am grieving ever having one, ever being a mum. This time felt very final. It changed my internal dialogue from one of worry about my fertility running out of time and desperateness for motherhood to one of utter despair.

My period was late, I knew it could be irregular after a miscarriage, so I had waited. I felt too exhausted to feel hopeful, too scared to feel excited. I didn't have the energy to go through another loss. I had taken a test. Negative. I was relieved and yet still crushed. How to describe this feeling? Of watching hope fade, like a distant smoke plume, becoming invisible as it mixes with the air around it.

3rd March 2018

My home feels like the dementors have moved in. I can't face fighting this again, it's so much effort. I need the energy to be normal for work. I can't stretch to finding hope and joy again too. In true Scarlet O'Hara fashion, I'll think about that tomorrow. Somehow, I always find the smile to complete the look by the time I get into the office, but I allow myself not to bother with it on the train in. Still no period. No baby either. Just my body messing with me.

I was trying really hard to bounce back. I couldn't just stop as much as some days I wanted to. If I could choose, I'd just stay on the sofa, curled up with my little Chloe and never move again. But I wanted to live and feel alive. I wanted to be an active member of life, not just watch it leave me behind. I felt like I had fallen off the merry-go-round of life and it was going too fast; I couldn't get back on. All I could do was watch it, trying to build up the energy to try and jump back on again.

I had been trying to think about what next? How do I get my family? I wouldn't accept defeat. Clearly it was not going to happen naturally. We talked about using a donor egg, but the Consultant at Guys had felt that miscarriage would always be the outcome of any pregnancy. I hadn't really taken his words to heart until now. Suddenly they boomed loudly in my mind. I couldn't face another miscarriage. Nor could we afford to keep doing IVF.

So, I started looking into surrogacy. It seemed that if you went via the right channels that it was safe enough. Neither of us were happy about the fact that you are not recognised as parents or legal guardians, even if the child is genetically ours, until after the birth. That was going to require a lot of trust. In the UK it's illegal to ask someone to carry a child for you, you have to wait to be offered. So, a surrogate has to like you. What pressure!

Surrogacy UK organise a lot of socials where you go along and meet and greet possible surrogates. The trouble is, I was not very sociable these days. Loss does that. I couldn't be bothered to 'get to know' anyone, happy chit-chat, pretending life is just peachy. I just lost my seventh baby. My child, which I loved. Some days it took everything just to crack a smile, or answer a call, in fact I avoided calls mostly, I couldn't engage with the world in that way yet. I was back to letting post pile up.

Reading post and having to absorb or deal with its contents, requires more energy than you realise. Meeting people and being chatty is the last thing I wanted to do. And yet, if someone has to choose us, then I have to be smiley, chatty, likeable.

They had an online forum also, which I was encouraged to join. In this group, I found a lovely group of people. I wrote an introductory note and received a lot of support. I felt like I'd found my people. These people understood the pain of feeling desperate for a family of your own, of having lost a baby, or more. Of seeing the world carry on around you whilst yours has stopped.

However, there were still reservations. It's a difficult thing, thinking that someone else may carry my child, I felt such sorrow at not being able to do this most basic of biological tasks, it should be like breathing, just part of what your body does. To know that stranger may then opt to not let me have my child afterwards felt extremely dangerous.

My Facebook profile picture was one of my cat, which had suited me fine for years. However, I realised we now needed to sell ourselves as this amazing couple, any surrogate would love to carry a child for. I hunted around to find a picture of us both, which would sell us as a couple. No easy task, we both have the Chandler Bing (from the Friends sitcom) syndrome, as soon as the camera is facing us, we grimace. The only good pictures are usually when we are not aware a picture is being taken, so finding a good one of us together, took some doing. I was in full-on PR mode. "Pick us!"

Although it's illegal in the UK to charge for surrogacy, a surrogate is allowed to charge expenses. Surrogacy UK told me to expect between £15,000-20,000 for one pregnancy. On top of that we'd have to pay the £6,000-7,000 required for IVF. I then read a lot of comments from people who had had a child via surrogacy and they said to expect closer to £45,000-£50,000, what with any time off work and travel for us, that's a terrifying amount. How could I save up for this? It would take decades.

Apparently, a surrogate can include a family holiday in their expenses. I don't even go on my own holidays because I've been saving so long for IVF, how could I then be expected to pay for someone else's? I fully appreciate it's a sacrifice, pregnancy is not without risks and to be a surrogate registered with Surrogacy UK, they have to have had at least one live birth, so they clearly have their own families, this was not a judgement on these women who do make a huge sacrifice, but it's a tough realisation that you are paying for a lifestyle you can't even allow yourself.

I was so conflicted, between really wanting a baby of my own and feeling like I'd be held over a barrel financially for it. Should we take a loan? What if it took several tries? What if we got into financial difficulties? I didn't want to put a price on motherhood. What price for joy? Who wouldn't do anything they could for ultimate happiness? And if I don't want to, if I'm not willing to put that much money towards it, then how much do I really want a baby? I didn't want to be judged. I felt if I decided against surrogacy, especially using the cost as an issue, people would think that of me, that I couldn't really have wanted children all that much.

I kept looking for a local social we could join, to meet some of the surrogates and other parents or intended parents who are also looking for a surrogate. It felt like it would be a popularity contest. It felt very pressured, but it also felt like a solution. I was enjoying chatting to a few of the women in the group. I realised some had been members of the group for a long time, which scared me. To be matched with a surrogate via Surrogacy UK, we would have to register and pay £800 for the privilege, even if we were never matched.

Finally, after several weeks of looking and waiting, a social in London was announced. It was quite a trek away, but I couldn't wait any longer, this needed to happen now. I signed us up.

Dreams

Dreams
So real they became me
Shattered
In pain
Mended by hope, joyful hope
Shattered
Once more
But hope returned
Unwavering, determined hope
Shattered
Demoted from absolute future to a wish
Unfailing hope springing back
Shattered
Again?
Dreams
Faint like ancient photographs
Tumbling like autumn leaves
Trampled
Rebuilt
Shattered
Dreams seemingly out of reach, and yet....
What joy is this?

Resilient Hope
Shattered
Twice
Hope is vanquished, silenced at last
Despair an easy replacement
No fight left
Who could go on? Why would you?
Time, healer or trickster?
Hope returns, like a glimpse of blue sky
on a stormy day
Ridiculous hope
Shattered
Dreams
Never truly disappear
But no longer joyful
Dreams have become waking
nightmares
If I pretend I don't care……
Dreams

February 2018

After losing the twins last year, watching television had become really difficult. I could no longer bear seeing any babies at all. So, we started watching the Walking Dead. I'd always wanted to watch it but had always been a bit too scared. But this was safe viewing, this was zombies. As I lost my seventh baby, one of the main characters was pregnant. I managed to ignore that as best I could, but suddenly, we got to the episode where the baby was born. Another programme I could no longer watch. We were running out of options.

I was terribly busy at work, which I think was a blessing. We were rolling out new IT equipment to the entire organisation (close to 40,000 staff), with new technology and facing a lot of resistance to this change. I had no time to think at all during the working day. Luckily, I was working with a great group of people, I actually enjoyed being at work. They helped so much, without even knowing. It was stressful, we were delivering a major programme across the whole organisation at considerable pace. It was huge, it was non-stop and yet the laughter, the jokes, the coffees and after work drinks kept us all going. It was one of those rare teams, that happen every once in a while, where everyone just gets on. Everyone could have a laugh and we all encouraged one another when it felt overwhelming. It helped at the time that they didn't know. I did later share my story with the team, but at the time I couldn't. It felt nice to just be part of the team, nothing unusual. "Nothing to see here".

One of the things which I found the hardest on this journey and with my grief, is my loss of a sense of self and identity. I was no longer who I thought I was. I make things happen and yet I couldn't influence this. I didn't like me much anymore and tried to ignore me as best I could. I think it was part of putting on my office face, I pushed the real me so far inside that I couldn't see or feel her anymore. I didn't want to. And yet without her, without me, what was I? How could I heal? Now I wonder if this loss of sense of identity is what made me feel like I was somehow separated from the living world by that pane of glass.

11 May 2018

Right now, I don't care how you come about, I just want you in my life. I suspect either way you will no longer be biologically mine. I just want my family, I want you. I want my tiny baby feet running around and the smell of baby hair. I want the full shebang. I want family meals, the mess, the arguments, the homework, the holidays, the Christmas movies under a blanket, the stressful days off work with sick kids.... the lot!

We were still officially trying, but our enthusiasm had waned through hurt, disappointment and dread. I was still desperate to get pregnant, and equally terrified about actually becoming pregnant. I wanted to meet one of my children, but I automatically assumed pregnancy would lead to another loss and I didn't think I had the strength to go through it again. I think I couldn't make that decision, to stop. That would be admitting defeat, but I didn't want to risk pregnancy either, so our 'trying' took a back seat, we found we were too tired, too busy, had an early meeting the next day. Any reason to not.

I had never become obsessed in the trying. I was distraught when it didn't work, but I'd never got into ovulation charts, taking temperatures, having hours when it was go, go, go, right now! I had always kept a track of my periods and from these, I could roughly guess when I might be more fertile in the month, but I didn't really know. We went with sex as often as possible over the month, which doctors I spoke to confirmed was plenty. It obviously had been to start with. Now our trying seemed to be the reverse tactic. As little as possible in the hope it wouldn't happen, but without having to admit the truth to ourselves, to one another, that it wouldn't happen.

Infertility is a strain on a relationship, sex becomes about making a baby, something I tried really hard to not allow to happen. However I don't think it's possible to go through fertility issues and it not be a factor. So much of normal couple life is impacted. Paulo would pick me up from the station some days and I would get into the car and sob. I would hold my tears in all day but the minute I was somewhere quiet, safe, I couldn't keep up the façade. He may have had a really tough day at work and rather than unwind on the way home, he had to watch my heart break. Every month when my period started, I would disappear into my own world of hurt, I was unreachable. Some days I didn't want to see anyone or do anything. Even though our relationship is close and remained so throughout our losses, I still felt very alone in facing my heartache. I am also aware that I respond to heartache by withdrawing. He was wonderful, he seemed to just know when to allow me to feel my grief and be in my own little world, but also when it was time to pull me back from the abyss of loss. He would try to make me laugh. Often, I resented his light-heartedness when I was hurting so much, but mostly he would end up succeeding.

We were due to go to our first Surrogacy social in late June. I'd been waiting for it to happen for months whilst dreading the pressure behind it. Finding a surrogate, being liked, being chosen. In the end it came up quite suddenly. This was going to be our answer. We got up, got dressed and started gardening with a need to do something with our nervous energy. I asked whether my boyfriend wanted to go, he didn't. He felt he didn't know enough about it. Initially I was angry, it's always down to me. I had been talking about this for months now. Then I realised, even with all my research, I didn't feel I knew enough about it either, because we didn't know our surrogate. We didn't know if we would ever find a surrogate, we didn't know if we could trust her if we did. We decided not to go, and I felt a weight lifted from me. This decision was more than about just today. We didn't want this. This wasn't the route for us, not now, maybe not ever. I cried the rest of the day, it felt like I was somehow letting go of my dream.

The days after deciding not to go to the social felt like that weird void you feel at a funeral. Barely contained grief with a public face on it. Numb. Wanting the day to end whilst not wanting the rest of life to start. Had we just said goodbye to ever having a baby, ever having a brand new, fresh from the womb baby? Was my motherhood itself now in question? I wondered if I was on the road to acceptance and letting go of my dream. I felt like I had got to a stage where I could no longer fight nature on this. I questioned it all, I felt so bereft, but of what? We'd not even started anything.

I stayed on the Surrogacy UK Facebook group, more just in case, because although it felt like our decision was final, we hadn't actually said it out loud. There hadn't been one reason we could pinpoint as to why we didn't want this. I had wanted this to be our answer. This could have been the perfect solution. I wondered if it was because I find being around pregnancy so painful. Would still be the case, even if the baby was eventually going to be mine? I actually think it still would. I loved being pregnant, I loved carrying my babies, every single minute. I loved how calm I felt. I loved having them with me, with all the horrid symptoms that came with it. I felt complete. Perhaps my view is skewed as to how likely it is to miscarry a baby, but the thought of paying for someone else's eggs to be carried by a third person, who we end up paying a lot of money to, for them to potentially also miscarry.....when is enough, enough?

5th July 2018

I don't want to give up or admit defeat, I want a family. I'm so tired of waiting and hoping. I'm tired of wanting. I'm tired of feeling a piece of me is missing, it's exhausting! I think it's time to change path. I'm trying really hard to not think of this as plan B, because my plan was always to be a family, it's the same plan, just a different route to it.

I know that any child who comes into my life I will love more than words. Even just little Chloe, I would do anything for her, she is completely my surrogate child, I fell in love with her. I have absolutely no worries about loving a child who comes to live with me. I worry they may not love me though.

I just need to feel like I'm moving forwards, I'm doing all I can. Christmas will be here before we know it, then my birthday, I'll be 43. 43 without a family? How could that be my life? You were supposed to be here such a long time ago. Well, forget you coming to me, I'm now coming to you, hold on my little one.

Plan A version 2.0

Following the conversation with the consultant from Guys, as well as other doctors and from my own research I suspected my miscarriages were my immune system attacking the foetus. It's not that they weren't meant to be, but that I was not able to carry them. I had all the tests which are carried out in the UK. I could have gone abroad to have more tests, but at what cost?

Again, I beat myself up, if I genuinely wanted a baby, I'd have done this. But they could all come back with nothing new. How much money do you throw at something before accepting it won't change anything? How many more years do I waste investigating something which may never change the outcome? I was out of fertile years. My need for motherhood and family hugely outweighs the need for it to be my own biological baby. Adoption more and more felt less like plan B, but the only option to Plan A and my happiness.

In July, we met with a social worker from the council we'd been recommended, in a café, after work. It all felt very casual. Odd location for that kind of discussion, but why not? We talked through our situation and what we wanted. She let us know that foster-to-adopt could mean that we have a long wait between children. If you have a new-born, you are then not deemed ready to adopt another child for many years. She warned it could take up to five years to have another child. I didn't want to be the mother of a new-born at 50, that wasn't fair on either the baby or me. I can already see a difference in how I bounce back from late nights compared to 10-15 years ago. There's a reason we're more fertile in our 20's! I hate this thought. I hate it because there is nothing I can do to change the fact that I am now well into my 40's with no children.

I struggled to understand the thinking behind this. I'm not being flippant, I know a new baby is hard work, I understand that, but in terms of attachment, they've not been through the upheaval of a child who has lived with birth parents and then foster parents, potentially more than one foster family, not to mention lived through some kind of abuse or neglect. An older child would surely come with potentially a whole host of behavioural and emotional issues. As someone with no children, I suspect a toddler is just as disruptive to your life as a new-born baby. Yes, they may sleep better, but very possibly not, especially if traumatised. A new house, new bedroom, living with brand new people they don't know, new routines. They will notice and react to the change. They need constant entertainment; they are draining in a different way. I didn't see how you can get two toddlers in quick succession, but not two new-born babies? I so wanted to live every possible moment with my children, so I didn't miss out on any of it. To feel like a complete mother. Their mother.

We kept chatting with this lady for over an hour. She told us in adoption circles, we were not old parents, both of us being 42. That didn't really help me, 40 had always been my cut-off. My mind went back to that conversation with my sister, when I must have been around eight or nine years old, that old parents always had square children. Oh no!

We told her that we wanted two children, I'd go for three, even four, I always wanted a big family, but Paulo wasn't so keen. We said we'd consider a sibling group, saying this out loud, it just clicked, this felt right. This was it. This was how we would have our family. For the first time in an exceedingly long time, I felt hope. I was filled with it. Suddenly the sun shone a little brighter, the trees were a bit greener, the sky was bluer.

The process would be slow, we had to attend an open session first and the first one we could attend was in September. Maybe we needed more time anyway. I think I was already onboard before this meeting, but Paulo was not instantly sold, and I think still hopeful for a natural conception.

After that first session, we would be allocated a social worker. The lady we spoke to sent us a reading list including films and podcasts. We started with the first, an easy one, a film called Lion. It was emotional. I felt sad that my child would always want to know their birth parents, like I'd never be quite enough. I understood the need to know where you come from, to find that connection to your past, to see a resemblance also, but it still hurt. I wanted my love to be enough.

The decision made, our way forwards paved, I felt I was moving forwards. I hoped that would make everything feel better, but there is no magic way of erasing pain, of wiping out the damage of infertility. We also still had a lot to learn about adoption itself. It was no walk in the park.

21st July 2018

Just finished reading one of the books. It's thrown me completely, I cried lots but also feel quite down, with the realisation that depending on how damaged the children are, I might not be able to go back to work, or not outside school hours anyway. How can I afford that?

It's so horrid, this couple adopted children aged one & three who had been in care for a while. They were neglected & the older one was abused. He remembered bits. He couldn't talk well at all because no one ever chatted to him, he spent hours alone. His prefrontal cortex, his attachments, all destroyed by his birth parents. It's heart-breaking.

Am I strong enough to deal with such broken little people?

My friend who had lost her baby at the end of last year was pregnant again. She was so considerate and had asked me whether I'd be ok being involved? I really, really wanted to be. I said yes that I did. She sent me a scan picture and it broke me. How could I feel so awful about something so joyful? Would I ever not be touched by this agonising grief? I just wanted everything to stop. Time to stop. Until everything was ok. But it doesn't stop. I think this is where I can now see the difference between my grief and my want for motherhood. We were working towards motherhood, we had a plan, it would happen. Therefore, I think the fact that these triggers still hurt was mostly linked to the losses I'd been through.

2nd August 2018

I started reading my second adoption book. She mentioned she felt betrayed by friends who get pregnant. I understand what she means. It does almost feel that way, as ridiculous as that sounds. As if there is a queue somewhere and they've jumped it. I know it makes no sense. I find it hard to have these feelings, which feel mean, but it actually felt nice reading that someone else has these ridiculous thoughts too. In that moment I felt less alone. Infertility is cruel. It feels like it's taken away some of my gentleness.

I had been working with bereaved people as a counsellor for a couple of years now. It's odd that we can show empathy to others and yet berate yourself for the very same. We would talk about their loss and how a deep loss doesn't just go away, you don't 'get over' it, you learn to live with it, carrying it with you. One of the hardest elements of loss is that life goes on. It's very difficult to accept. I knew this, I could see this resonated with my clients and we would work towards that acceptance for them and yet I was expecting myself to just move on and get over it. I didn't know how.

I hated that I felt so alone. I kept looking for forums, for answers, for comfort. I would have some of my feelings validated. "Losing a baby is massive no matter how far along you were"; "It's not just a baby, it's the child that baby would become, the adult they would be"; "Another child can never replace the lost child", but then the lady who'd posted her story would mention another child, even several other children, or she would mention she was coming up to her 30th birthday and my sense of connection would evaporate. I seemed to be the only one who was entirely childless, who was 'old'. I was the only one on these forums who was out of time. My only option was outside of me. Surrogacy didn't feel right, adoption felt unreal and far off. I just felt more alone. I didn't fit in with any category.

5th August 2018

Another journey into work fighting tears. And it does feel like a fight.

It was a difficult day, my period was a few days late, so I allowed myself to dream. Even nipped out at lunchtime to get a test. Only for my period to start almost the minute I got back to my desk....as if just taunting me!

Then we met the adoption lady again after work. We discussed the fact that we were having a loft conversion and extension. To adopt two children, you need to have three bedrooms, so the children can have one each. We didn't, we had one and a half, or one and a box room.

She said we'd not be able to complete the second part of the process until the loft conversion was complete. I was hoping we could do it alongside, so that the house and the approval were ready at the same time! Bearing in mind we've only just put in for the planning permission, which could take four months in itself. Then add to that the actual build. It will be at least a year from now just to get to the approval stage, let alone matched to children. Another year waiting.

So, then maybe we should move, but that would cost considerably more, and we've not even thought about where to move to. I think if we moved, we would look outside of London, but we would need to still be able to get to work. Where do we start looking? Also, with our house as it is now, we would not get the amount that we would need for a three-bed house.

I went to visit my mum that August. We talked about adoption. I talked about some of the books I'd been reading and what the children had gone through. My mum was always so kind and empathetic, she said that she knew I would be able to look after these children. It felt reassuring. My mum had not been my go-to to discuss things with for a very long time now, talking with her isn't always easy, but sometimes she's fully there and I get a sense of how our relationship was. I always knew that she would be fine with adoption. I knew that for her, any child I loved and looked after would be her grandchild. She would never have been the sort to struggle with this idea, she would have accepted any child I had by whatever means. I felt sad that she wouldn't be closer to my children, both physically because she lived abroad, but also emotionally.

11 September 2018

I'm a mess, I wake up feeling like I'm under a boulder and I can't breathe. I'm not sure what triggered it? The baby thing never goes away. The memory of all of them haunt me. For such a long time I had flashbacks just going to the toilet in my own home. Remembering the pain, the blood. Remembering begging my babies to stay. Feeling so desperate to hold onto them and guilty that I couldn't keep them safe.

And it's coming up to Christmas.... again....and I'm not a mum.... again. I'm starting a New Year no further forwards than I was last year, or the year before, or the year before that, and yet I've had such a struggle trying to. A New Year also means my birthday, I'm a year older and still there is no change. I know that's all very tunnel vision, I just can't see past it some days. Just stuck in an endless loop of non-motherhood year after year after year. I hate the repetition of it.

The home visit

We went to the adoption session at the end of September. The room was cold, even though it was a sunny day. It was full of couples. Are they competition? Do we need to stand out at this point? A couple came to give a talk about their adoption journey, I was so excited and tearful. This felt tangible. This could happen for me. It felt far more achievable than a successful pregnancy. If I could only rush through the building works. Awful how much of the time I spend wishing my life away, when life is so precious.

The move to adoption feels like one step forwards, two back. I feel at last that I'm taking positive action, action which will make motherhood a reality for me, but it also feels more far away, as if it may never really happen. At least if you are trying to physically have a child, by whatever means, your body is involved. Adoption all feels very theoretical, separate to me.

The following Monday on the train to work, opposite where I stood, was a pram with a beautiful baby girl. She had a little Disney scarf on her head and was quietly sucking her dummy. Her eyes stared out sleepily at nothing in particular. I so wanted to take out my phone and take a picture. To immortalise that beautiful, serene little face. To remember what it felt like to just look at her. The joy her little sleepy face bought, just by being there on the tram with me. My heart felt heavy and tears threatened as I looked at her longingly. I can't take her picture, she's not mine to look at or love. I wonder if this feeling will go, when I have my children? Will they feel like mine, or will I feel the same, that these are not mine to truly love? I so hope seeing a young baby will become easier. My children won't be very young babies. I will have missed out on the very beginning of their lives. Will that still feel like a gap, or will the fact I am a mother calm the sorrow I feel?

28 September 2018

It's crazy how wanting something so badly can make your mind think any number of nonsense. Yesterday I had the worst migraine. I felt almost paralysed. I found it difficult to move, my whole right side felt heavy. I'd all but stopped having migraines until I got pregnant. Now, they seem to happen just before a period, as well as after. That ridiculous hope of mine, keeps popping up. I didn't take anything for the pain, just in case I might be pregnant.

Then last night, my period started, only lightly, but I didn't want to take anything for the cramps, just in case it wasn't really a period, but attachment bleeding. Because after all these months of nothing, that would happen! I love that hope is such a powerful emotion, but it doesn't half play with your emotions in the process. That's two days needlessly lost to pain.

I just want my babies back. I still can't believe they've gone. I want to be pregnant again. Pick up where we left off. I want to actually meet one of my babies. Look into their eyes. Stroke their little soft cheek. Hear their cry. I'd do anything to hear my baby's voice.

I kept on looking for similar stories, trying to find someone I could relate to, someone whose journey mirrored my own. I wanted to not feel so alone. It had been tough reading many of the adoption books, people write them once they had their children. The same with books on IVF or any other sort of infertility issues, people wait for the happy ending to have happened before writing. So, by then, their wounds are healed, or healing. Their books become all about the happy ending, not the journey to it. I didn't recognise myself in these stories, just more happy families, which I couldn't relate to yet. They did provide some glimpses to my story, but invariably it had been a shorter journey with less loss and they'd reached the destination of parenthood a lot faster, which made me feel so alone and such a failure.

Following our start down the adoption route, I felt that my outlook has started to shift. It had given me somewhere for the hope to go without feeling caged by despair as it had been. I felt like my children were out there, just out of reach now. I already loved my children, I just needed to meet them. It had given me a glimmer of hope that my end is in sight. It made me feel a lot less angry at the unfairness. Maybe also the beginnings of being able to find me again. The nice me. The one not consumed with anger and grief.

However, my initial feeling that starting adoption meant we were moving forwards was soon eclipsed by the fact we had to wait months. My usual triggers hadn't just vanished and now it felt as if we were treading water again. My periods came and went accompanied by the usual tears. An opportunity lost. It was so familiar it was almost boring. Biology has let me down again. I remember during biology lessons, finding out that life always finds a way. What a joke. It turns out life had hit a dead end with me.

11th Oct 2018

The shame of feeling jealous of other losses. Ridiculous. With baby loss day coming up, there are lots of posts, of people losing a baby through stillbirth. Those babies are recognised, their birth and death are recorded. The parents have memory boxes, very often photos and a little memorial service. They existed and were real. The parents can justifiably feel bereaved. They have lost a baby.

I've seen the term 'born still but still born', which is beautiful and must be very comforting for those parents, but it cuts me like a knife. My loses were all within the first three months. They don't count to the outside world. They would be classed as medical waste had they happened in hospital. There is no recognition. No birth certificate, no funeral. No memory box with photos. No baby to mourn. I was not a mother.

The miscarriage clinic wouldn't even let me have a copy of the scans of my babies when I asked. It's the only evidence I have that they even existed, and I wasn't allowed a copy. I'm allowed a copy of my blood test results, but not evidence of my babies. Their pictures. I'm just a patient and my pregnancies just stopped. I threw all the tests away at the time, since I'd peed on them. Now I wish I'd kept them. Proof.

My babies have all been so real to me. They were wanted so desperately and loved from the first moment. They became my everything immediately. I did everything to protect them, no tea or coffee, none of the forbidden foods. I even walked slowly; I hate walking slowly! The love and connection I felt for my babies was so profound. They were part of me.

I finally contacted the same seller I got my bracelet from and got three additional little birthstones. She sent a very sweet message saying sorry they were required (it was a baby-loss site).

I hate what I've become, just this ball of grief and pain. I want to be that girl who felt that she'd be fine with a miscarriage, because this meant the baby wasn't meant to be, for whatever *reason. I'm not her. I'm sad. I think my babies were meant to be; I was the problem. I want my babies back. I want my heart in one piece.*

I thought about the fact that one in four pregnancies ended in miscarriage. Which means that out there, there are 27 women who had babies, whilst I lost all 7 of mine. I still find the unfairness suffocating.

I was invited to my friends' hen do. She was in the last trimester of her pregnancy and I was dreading it. I loved my friend dearly, but being around a pregnancy filled me with dread. I couldn't not go. I sat next to her in the restaurant, the familiar feeling of a magnet pulling my uterus towards the baby, such an uncomfortable pulling sensation, which may be psychological, but feels entirely physical. I wanted to hold my stomach, as if by magic, it contained a baby. I wanted to cry. I smiled and laughed and joined in. And drank a lot of champagne. I got home and collapsed in sobs in the hall, my legs unable to hold the weight of my grief to make it further into the house.

The loss still felt so raw sometimes. I judged myself for being angry, for being jealous. For still not having processed the losses. For needing to acknowledge them. I'm sure many people thought I should have moved on by now. I know I did.

I think many who have not been through infertility, assume the struggle is just that you can't have a baby. For me, infertility is not simply the lack of a baby. Yes, that's the obvious, visible thing missing. But a family is so much more. It's a life, a continuation, a generation in your family. Imagine if your grandparents had been infertile, no you, no cousins, just a dead end. I don't want to be a dead end. It's about being loved, being remembered, meaning something to someone. Having a legacy.

It's also the little things, the birthday cards, nursing sick children, making them their favourite dinner when they get better. Holding a hand to cross the road. Trying to rush somewhere with a toddler who has no sense of time. Everyday life. Going for days out, which they find boring, but, if they're anything like me, will form some very fond memories of childhood and leave lasting in-jokes about your mum spending more time in the gift shop than she ever did in the exhibition.

Infertility also has such a huge impact on relationships, with yourself, your partner, your family, your peers and your relationship with society. For me it's been having people I loved surrounding me and yet feeling very alone. It's been not recognising myself in my thoughts. Its avoiding situations or having to muster huge amounts of courage to face a situation which should be fun. Its feeling like you have failed an amazing man who would be the best dad. It's a grief, sometimes for babies lost, but even without miscarriage, its grief for babies not had, not held. Motherhood not achieved. An expectation not fulfilled. Defunct biology.

Early in October, two social workers from the Council came to visit us at home. They talked to us both for three hours. They asked about everything, how we had come to adoption, everything about our relationship, our families, our medical histories. It was intense, a little intrusive, but understandable. They wanted to get a picture of who we were. We were both honest. We spoke about our lost babies. Paulo got quite choked up talking about them. I'd been seeing my counsellor and gone all round the houses with my feelings on the matter, as well as speaking to friends about it, but he'd not really spoken to anyone about it.

Meanwhile, I hadn't entirely given up the biological route. Or, in hindsight, I wasn't ready to accept the reality. I went to see my doctor about maybe taking Clomid, a drug which helps with ovulation, to see if that could boost my egg count. I mean I fell pregnant, maybe I've just not got enough eggs now? My doctor said she couldn't refer me for this because of my age, being over 40. Punishment for having waited so long, I guess. However, she said she could refer me because of my endometriosis, and I could mention Clomid at the appointment. She was very sweet, she smiled at me and said, "never give up". She understood.

26th October 2018

There was a picture on the surrogacy site today, a mother and a baby. It made my eyes water. Sometimes it's so difficult to explain why I want a family and children so, so much. I suspect after all the miscarriages and hurt I've been through some may think I should give up already. The picture I saw explained it so much better than my words ever could. I'm missing out on THE greatest gift, on my reason of being.

Today we got the answer from social services and I have been sobbing all day. It was what I was expecting, but their wording is so poor. We are apparently 'not ready to adopt'. That is so untrue! And a complete lie too. But we can't say anything. We need to play the game; these people have my future in their hands. We are ready! So, we got upset talking about losing seven babies. Could anyone not? The only reason my upset was deemed ok, is that I said I'd seen a counsellor. He didn't, so he needs to see one. He is so much more together than I am.

We were also told we need to stop trying. I have a friend who got pregnant whilst they were going through the adoption process (she was approved), but they lied about trying.

This is obviously what we should have done. Although she was considerably younger than I am now. This feels like such a huge ask.

We talked about adoption and agreed that even if we did get pregnant now, we'd still adopt. I wouldn't want an only child and with my age, I would be lucky for one miracle, let alone two. But to stop trying? That's like giving up.

It feels like such a massive rejection. Like I'm not good enough to adopt. I can't keep my own babies; I cannot be worthy of anyone else's.

Adoption really was my last means of motherhood. If I couldn't do this, it really would all be over. I wouldn't let that happen, they said we weren't ready, not that we weren't suitable. They want us to confirm we are definitely no longer trying. They want us to see a counsellor. We will do these things. The stopping trying, well we all but had. I am so excited about our little sibling group. I can't help but imagine the family we would be. Then I worry about how broken my children would be. But I can't help but picture Christmas day, excited little faces. I know there is more to family than Christmas, that's just my focal point.

23rd November 2018

Time does help. I didn't want it to. I didn't want to let go of the pain which is my only remaining link to my babies. But the rawness does ease up. It's not constant. I have times when the pain washes over me and the intensity hasn't diminished at all, but it doesn't last as long and is easier to recover from.

Today I feel resigned to the pain. I'm accepting it's always going to be there in some shape or form. Even when I am a mum, and my ache for motherhood is a thing of the past, I think I will still have moments of grief for my babies. Now, I think I'll share this grief with my children, who will probably always feel a sense of loss for not living with their birth mum. We will both have our grief, but together have the most amazing family and hopefully heal more strongly together.

I still feel like I have a dual life, normal, smiley self at work and with friends but when I stop, I just feel empty. My social life has bounced into life, as it always does towards the end of the year. It's like people suddenly realise they need to see one another. I am just as guilty of this; I try to get in a catch up with all my friendship groups before Christmas. It does make it very busy. Especially now because of the effort involved in maintaining 'normal' me. It feels extra busy. It also feels so surreal. The last two Christmases I was pregnant and two years previously also, and yet still I face a childless Christmas. I don't know which is worse, the loss of my darling, desperately loved and wanted babies or the complete lack of hope I feel facing exactly the same childless Christmas again?

I had not called up about the scan, which I needed ahead of seeing the gynaecologist about maybe taking Clomid. I kept berating myself, asking how much I can really want a child if I can't even book a simple scan. Yet I felt so traumatised by scans. I'd had so many scans, tests, hospital appointments, most of which led to bad news at best, the heartache of there being no heartbeat at worst. I just couldn't bring myself to.

I read an article about endometriosis and its link to infertility and felt like I'd been punched in the stomach. Why did I never discuss my painful periods with a doctor. People talk about period pains, I assumed that was all it was. I could have had it treated years ago, before it killed off one of my ovaries. I was frustrated I hadn't known. It may not have changed anything, just increased my chances of pregnancy, and you never know, one may have got through? Although being single during my 30's had just as big, if not a bigger impact and you can't make life send you Mr Right, for me unchosen and unwanted singledom was also part of my infertility journey.

12th December 2018

Today, my period started, and I'm devastated, so what's new I hear you sigh? I had night sweats, remembered dreams and had a migraine. I managed to convince myself maybe......? I mean around Christmas seems to be when I am pregnant a lot, why not believe there's something in the time of year that is favourable? Why not hope? Well this morning is why, I'm crushed. I can't face the day. My body seems to deceive me very cruelly. More to the point, why did I believe it would be any different? Hope is supposed to see you through to a better day, give you courage. Hope kills me.

The day approaches once more. I really hate Christmas. My favourite day of the year. I read a post on the Dovecote (childless support organisation) page, with a poignant piece of writing, which is quite long, but starts 'somewhere tonight a woman sitting next to her Christmas tree, year after year her heart tells her it's another Christmas without children, and as the tears roll down her sweet face she swears next year will be different'. This could have been written by me! It's how I feel every year, and what I promise myself each year also. It was beautiful and made me cry. It ends up being religious, which I am not, and I feel that ruins the ending slightly, for me, but it's still such a beautiful piece. I hate that others feel as broken as I do, but it is so comforting to not feel so alone.

This year, we're with Paulo's family, which is very lively and I enjoy the experience of not having the weight of years of expectation on me, making it feel hard to breathe. I've not celebrated Christmas with these people before. Its liberating to not feel I should have progressed with life in the expected way, marriage, babies, normal life. I feel quite light without this pressure bearing down on me.

27th December 2018

This limbo, between Christmas and New Year. The first hurdle of facing the family orientated days with a smile is over, now, to accept another year, another start with my broken soul. I feel such emptiness. I don't know what to do with myself. Feels like grief, an inability to get involved. A desire to avoid life, to not need to speak to anyone. I was watching a Christmas movie earlier, where the lead character gets pregnant. The joy as the family celebrate the addition to their family. No thought that this joy may not happen. It's just assumed, you fall pregnant, you have a baby. I was dumbstruck by the thought that this is the norm. A positive pregnancy test means a baby. The tears in the father's eyes thinking about being a dad. I remember our first pregnancy test together, taken before work. The joy that we were having a baby, my boyfriend getting emotional on his way into work. The awful guilt that I've inflicted this much pain to this wonderful man.

This is something else I can berate myself about, along with the fact I am still hurting. I'm not 'being positive'. I'm not 'over' it. I am still 'going on' about my pain, my losses, my lack of motherhood. I should be fine now. Or at least, so used to this being my life that I should stop talking about it already.

We're adopting, our family is coming, I should be able to just draw a line under all the hurt, all the waiting.

Forget about the years I've missed out on my children's' lives, on your life. You. I've not written to you in such a long time. It's like I've stopped believing you will ever really be here, be a real child.

Still on my quest to heal and find peace, to find myself again, I keep looking for something soothing, a quote or a book that could help me. I keep coming across quotes, such as 'hard times are often a blessing in disguise' going on to say, 'sometimes the hardest lessons to learn are the ones your spirit needs most'. I mean who writes this stuff? How can my spirit ever need the lesson of losing a baby? Seven times. I didn't think there could possibly be a lesson here. Other than to not expect what everyone else gets. To not feel worthy of joy. Along with many other quotes about sorrows making you stronger, or one I'd seen a lot is that 'God only gives you what you can deal with'. I didn't want to be strong. I wanted to be just a normal person, with a perfectly ordinary life. Why should the fact I could deal with things mean that I deserved them to happen? Then there's also the quotes about everything happens for a reason. I've had a few people actually say that to me. The cheek! I'd like to know what good reason they could think of, for me to lose 7 babies? I've also had people try to cheer me up with the knowledge that my babies were too beautiful for earth. Firstly, as a non-believer, this made absolutely no sense to me, there is no other location they could be residing in. Secondly, I'd seen some pretty hot people on this earth. As well as some exceedingly good and virtuous ones, why would these people not also be too beautiful for this earth? Or do people who say this believe that my babies would have been even more amazing? Come on, they'd be little me's, scruffy but cute.

These types of quotes make me so angry. They are obviously directed at those who maybe have a choice in what has happened to them, or who maybe wait for things to come to them. That's not me. I took action. I tried, I'd fought so hard already, for everything I had. I fought so long to find love, I fought to have a baby, and fought and fought. I didn't know how to keep finding the strength to get up and fight again the next day. I didn't want to be strong. I wanted to just be bog-standard. I didn't want anything extraordinary.

Maybe I should just have appreciated them for what they are, people trying to comfort a hurt that makes no sense. It's hard when you're so embedded in the hurt to realise that others don't know how to deal with it either, or what to say. When you feel so lost yourself, you look outside for support, for that strength because you don't have it. But people don't know how to. Part of me thought they were just glad it hadn't happened to them.

I envied those who still had options, were using a surrogate or could use donor eggs. My reality felt starker, more final. From my point of view, you carried them, or got them on the day of their birth, either way they were 100% yours. No one else could lay claim to that child. Ever. I won't ever be their mum from day one. I will always share the motherhood of my children with another woman. They may have lived with her, remember her, love her. This truth hurt and was difficult to digest. It is frightening to face IVF and the concept or using donor eggs or sperm. These felt like luxuries to me now. My worry was how broken my children will be and how I can explain their past to them? I worried that I would always be a stand-in mum in their eyes. They would be my only children, but I wouldn't be their only mum. This broke my heart. I had waited so long for motherhood; I felt like I had been robbed of its completeness.

My children may look for their birth mum and she may have had genuine reasons for having had to give them up. She could be lovely. She could be everything they always dreamed their birth mum would be. And she would not be me. I would have to live with never living up to the dream of a biological mum. My children would never be fully mine. They would always have been someone else's first and would always have that strong connection to the start of their lives. To the one who gave them life.

Christmas over, onto the New Year. 2019. Another year, I couldn't believe it. I had been on this journey such a long time already. This year was going to be different; I had big plans. I was going on my first ever long-haul flight, to New Zealand. Besides the dread of the flight, I could not wait for this adventure. I had wanted to go there for such a long time.

This year our house would become a lot bigger. This year also, we were starting the adoption process. I wanted it to start now, but perhaps we needed the time. Besides, they wanted us to read more, to see a counsellor about our losses. We needed to tick these things off the list.

It did somehow feel closer, my goal of being a mum, of having my babies. Pregnancy had just led to loss and my motherhood getting dragged further away from me. It was so lovely to think they were out there. I felt as if I could field all my stored-up, overflowing love in their direction. I had no idea where they were, what they looked like, how old they were, but I loved them, and I couldn't wait to have them with me, to be their mum.

Not chasing parenthood

I recently watched Dynasties (David Attenborough), the one about penguins. Their desire to look after a baby leads those who are not paired up to hold a snowball under their fur, as they would a baby. Those with babies, if they should lose it, through hunger or cold, their need to nurture a baby is so strong they go out and try to take someone else's. It's not just a human pain, it's an animal pain. A life pain. Not being able to have or to keep a baby that you desperately want goes against nature.

I can relate to these penguins. I am a mum without a baby. Like that penguin who just wanted a baby to nurture, its all I wanted, its all I could think about and the heartache of missing my babies consumed me. The pain of having a piece of me missing was constant. I was starting to heal, the pain felt less debilitating, but as I've continued to heal since then, I can see that I was actually still drowning in grief. I guess in comparison to how I had been, I was doing considerably better. With grief I think you initially feel that you will never feel better, that's certainly how it felt for me. That the pain would never leave. It feels like you are in a constant state of high alert, unable to see past your loss. Therefore even a slight improvement feels monumental, feels like you're through it. Its only when you have reached a new level of healing that you can look back and see how broken you still were before. Even when, at the time you felt like you were 'better' because you'd come through the previous darkness, you could see some light, assuming that was the end of the tunnel, when it was really just a small window.

I recently read that there is a word for losing a partner, there is a word for losing parents, but there is no word for losing children. I'm not sure if this is because it's just a rare occurrence, deemed not important enough to acknowledge. The death rate of children under the age of 5 was pretty high for a huge part of our human history and still is in various countries around the world. Or, because it is just a pain beyond words. It's the wrong way around, you shouldn't die before your child. I'd never really thought about the lack of a word, but it's odd there isn't one. If there was a word for having lost a pregnancy, perhaps I wouldn't feel like my sorrow wasn't justified. Perhaps I could own up to my 'secret' motherhood, it would be validated. When I am asked "do you have children?" I could say, I'm a .... I wouldn't need to explain.

My childlessness was still ever present. I still could see no end to it. Adoption still felt so far away, just another pipedream as pregnancy had once been. My hope for pregnancy although fragmented, remained. Maybe, just maybe, a miracle might happen. I hadn't let that go yet.

6th February 2019

My period is now five days late. I do feel a bit sick in the morning, but I also feel exhausted. Still, I've not had any coffee all week at work just in case. Very unlike me. I don't have any other symptoms, no raging migraine, hot flushes and manic dreams I've had every time. But I did have a couple of dreams last week. I have convinced myself that I must be pregnant. This is it. Because I stopped trying, my mind was fixed on adoption.

The most annoying saying of "it'll happen when you least expect it" has come true. Annoying. But I'll take it on the chin if I am pregnant. There I said it. I've not dared pee on a stick yet, to not tempt fate, or burst this bubble I'm in. I've not berated myself for taking the lift either. I need to take it easy, keep you safe. Just over a year since I lost my last baby, that makes sense. My body needed to recover; I've not got a lot of eggs. I can take those odds. How amazing, you are coming to New Zealand with us. That will make it an even better trip. We'll be able to show you the photos in years to come - you were there, in my tummy.

7th February 2019

I bought the test. May as well know if I'm giving up coffee for a worthy cause. I've also had a shocking headache all day and the tiger balm isn't cutting it at all. I needed to know if I can take some decent drugs. So, I got home and took the test. A line starts to appear. It'll become two in just a second. I wait. That one line just gets stronger and stronger. The other one must still be just a bit too faint. I look closer. Nothing. It's probably not had enough time. I wait. Nothing. I put the test back in its wrapper and leave the bathroom. Paulo asks, "nothing?" I nod. What was I expecting? Well definitely not a baby!

The rest of the evening is wasted. I don't watch telly. I don't concentrate on messages from friends. I don't feel like eating. Silent tears fall as I try to eat dinner. Paulo lovingly wipes them from my cheeks. We've been here so many times, he knows there is not a thing he can say or do right now. After a time, I can't even bare being awake. I can't bear feeling. I escape to the bedroom. But there is no escape. My empty womb, my aching arms, my broken heart, my shattered dreams, my unfulfilled self, my silent, all-encompassing guttural scream of pain, from the very pit of my heart, all just follow me wherever I go. Not pregnant. Again.

It seems the more miscarriages you have, the more confused your body is. That, or it takes pleasure in messing with my fragile state of mind. My last period, in January also played tricks on me. I thought maybe it was a Christmas miracle as I lay unable to sleep for the third night in a row, feeling like I was on fire. These are not things which I ever had with my periods, for the first 26 of my menstruating years. The cruelty of my body. Not keeping my babies alive. Making me think there is another baby. It's like being tortured from the inside.

12th February 2019

I'm always searching and I'm not sure what for. I think for a reason, for solace, comfort, for some kind of understanding or closure to my pain. Did I really have to go through so much grief? Grief which has changed me, changed the very core of me. Grief which has felt too heavy to carry. Grief which I feel will stay with me for the rest of my life?

I felt split on social media. I understood it could offer support and increase awareness on many subjects, as well as just keeping us in contact with friends. But it could also open wounds. The support can be huge and I think by avoiding Social Media for so long for fear of being triggered, I lost a lot of opportunities when I was at my lowest, to be able to reach out to others who understood. But whilst the support can be huge, so can the triggers and the upset they can cause, which could at times take me days to recover from.

One evening, I saw three accounts, one from the surrogacy group, a woman who joined at the same time as I had, has been matched and had several attempts already with her surrogate. Then another contact who had successful IVF abroad. Finally, there was an article on a lady who met up with a daughter she gave up for adoption years before. She and the daughter had the biggest smiles on their faces.

All of these are heart-warming stories, but they all broke my heart. The surrogacy and IVF stories made me wonder if I had missed a trick. I could have tried harder. Should have tried harder. It's so difficult to know what is available, and what your next step should be. Anything the doctors told me I did. There is no one definitive tick list. There are simply options. I paid for three rounds of IVF. It's expensive. I questioned whether I should have taken loans, or gone abroad for tests or treatment. Even though the consultant felt I was rejecting my embryos and therefore I would also reject a donor embryo, I still thought I should have tried something else. I hadn't accepted yet that I had run out of road on this one. I felt I had let myself down. Now I see it wouldn't have changed anything. I'm sure from what I know now, that I would have miscarried anyway. It was self-preservation to stop. My choice was motherhood and the route I was pursuing was breaking me. I needed to keep in mind I fought for motherhood, not for a baby. Biology may have lost the battle, but motherhood would win.

To think some people only have to sleep with their partners to get pregnant and only have to get pregnant to have a baby. Imagine! The annoying people who enjoy 'trying' for a baby, because the trying is fun. Except when it's met with month upon month, upon year, of failure or when it is a success, it quickly turns into tragedy. Then 'trying' becomes more of a Russian roulette of emotions. Who gives up first? These people do not agonise over whether they tried everything or tried enough. Whether spending tens of thousands more on other treatments, other clinics, other tests, would have changed any outcome.

The third story, about the child put up for adoption being reunited with their birth mum brings a whole different heartache. Of course, any child reunited with a birth mother is going to have the broadest smile. That's their inner most desire. That's the dream. Even if their parenting left a lot to be desired, a child must still dream of the parent turning over a new leaf, learning, growing and coming back for them. Where does that put me? The person who did nurture and care for them as they should have been cared for. The person who waited so long to love them. The person who has seen first-hand this little person become who they should be. Do I ever belong in that smile? That smile of feeling like you're home. I knew I would love my adopted children as if they were mine, that isn't something I have ever questioned. But I wanted my adopted child to love me as they would their birth mother. And if they didn't, did that make me a stand in? A caretaker-mother? It was hard to think this is all I can ever be now.

There are different losses associated with adoption. There are rights of passage to parenthood which we won't experience, the birth, mums always compare birth stories. But also, as a couple. There's an amazingness in giving life which men seem to be in awe of, their wife or partner suddenly takes on the role of miracle worker. We won't have that moment as a couple.

Another is choosing the right name for your baby. With adoption now, changing the names of children is discouraged, rightly so, since the name is their identity and often the only part of it they can take with them. It belongs to them. We also won't have members of the family seeing likenesses of one or the other of us in our children, not to mention themselves or long-lost distant cousins, which give a family its sense of heritage and togetherness. My children in turn won't see their resemblance in their family. I will need to find other ways to give our story the roots to enable a deep family connection.

However, I find that as time goes on, I feel less of a loss over these things, because there will absolutely be a magic in how we build our own unique little pack. I feel already that we will find the children we were meant to have. A little in the same way my tutor once told me we get the clients we need as a therapist. I'm excited about starting our own traditions. Our family heritage will incorporate both of our families, but it will be our own. There is a huge freedom in this thought. There is a quote I have seen which I love "no snowflake ever falls in the wrong place". I think that will be our family motto. For one who doesn't believe in destiny, I could almost be fooled into thinking the right children will end up with the right parents. Souls meant to be together.

My fears may be entirely wrong, my children might adore me as the mum who was always there for them. They might soothe my brokenness. They might be the gold to seal the cracks of my broken heart, in the Japanese way of mending things 'Kintsukuroi' as I hope I am the gold to mend theirs. We may not have started off a matching set, but we'd certainly end up looking like it.

In a way, that feels almost more magical than the boring and ordinary way of creating children, without effort, without any sense of loss. Loss brings life into such sharp focus, our family will be forged by strength and resilience and love. So much love. The magic will be in our togetherness. A little like something is always sweeter when you've had to strive to achieve it or save up to buy it.

Paulo and I left for our adventure in New Zealand. The flight was fine, I surprised myself at how little I even thought about the fact I was flying, for 24 hour. We had an incredible time in New Zealand, I think we both needed a change of scene. A change of pace. We needed to be us. Not chasing parenthood, just us. A breather. The duration of our relationship so far had centred around having a baby and we had lost 6 babies together over 4 years. It had been tough and relentless and there was a very real risk of losing sight of us. Amazing us.

The trip had not been entirely without some reminders. We'd had a few difficult conversations over there, one gentleman had asked my boyfriend if we had children and when he replied no, the gentleman asked why? Infertility to those who don't know it, is like a black hole. He must have assumed the only reason someone wouldn't have a child would be through choice. I also had a gentleman talk to me about his grandchild and how lucky they were to have him, since at his mother's age, it's not easy. The mother in question is a couple of years younger than me. My biological clock made an awful toneless clanging chime at these words. These people didn't mean to wound, so we just smiled and nodded, whilst feeling completely winded by their comments. Why would they ever think we had lost so much?

I've said it before, but infertility has changed me, it has been long, heart-breaking and my thoughts and feelings so endlessly repetitive. It never goes away, it never leaves you. Everyday situations take on a very different perspective. Those who have not lost a baby or a part of themselves don't seem to truly grasp just how painful this loss is. There is still judgement on grieving for a miscarriage, it, along with the grief of childlessness, is still a disenfranchised grief. Not recognised by those who have not felt it. I felt like I had a baby from the moment I knew I was pregnant. In my heart and my mind I lost a baby, a real, living, breathing baby that I'd simply not met yet.

To know that for many this grief is dismissed felt like an added insult, like having your future snatched away from you wasn't enough of an insult. It felt as if the world felt my babies weren't real when my heart knew different. As if there is a stage during pregnancy when a woman suddenly feels a connection to her unborn child. I felt that connection immediately. If that stage existed, then a baby would only become real to its mother at that stage, not before. Mostly, I question whether there is any stage when a woman would be ok to lose a pregnancy and I'm fairly certain that is never, so the babies are real all along and should be recognised as such. If the babies are real, then the loss is real and this should be better recognised.

I would also like childlessness to be recognised as a severe, existential loss. Society has always been harsh to women who didn't fit the norm. The terms spinster and barren are shrouded in shame and accusation, like either of these are your fault. There is so much cultural expectation around bearing a child, providing an heir. Your status is linked to your success in this matter. This sounds very Victorian and yet having been on the receiving end of this 'failure', popular opinion has not moved on much.

The insensitivity of the first doctor I saw, asking me if I didn't like men, was so wounding at a time when I felt the problem was not me not liking men, but men not liking me. I felt rejected by the whole of mankind. My confidence was so low but I was trying to be proactive, to achieve my dream, to fulfil my purpose as a woman, as a living being. Like the penguins, I knew that I needed to have a chick to nurture and love. Its not just the doctor, I think this is what was least understood about my grief. People could understand losing a baby may be a sad event, even though they may not have understood the extent of that sadness, but the grief of being childless went unnoticed and unacknowledged. Over the years, I faced far more insensitive remarks about this than I ever did about my miscarriages. Sometimes from people close to me, who knew my story. This is another reason I wanted to share my story, to raise awareness of this very lonely experience.

I feel like my silence would be complicit in the lack of recognition of both the pain of childlessness and of baby loss. I feel like my pain was made worse and lasted longer because I didn't accept it or allow it. I felt it was unacceptable. My counsellor helped me so much with his acceptance and I feel I need to pass that on, pay it forward. Sharing my difficult journey may help those who have not experienced it understand how it feels. I really hope it can provide some comfort to those who have, that they are not alone.

Loss has altered most of my relationships, most noticeably the one I have with myself. I saw myself as a failure. I blamed myself. So much so that I stopped even seeing me. I no longer felt connected to the person looking back at me in the mirror. I will never again be the person I was before, but I can feel I am healing. Slowly for sure. Some days I still have to scrape myself up, off the floor. Some days it still takes all the energy I have just to act normal when I feel so broken. These days happen less and less frequently. I feel joy again. Often. I love being alive. I have hope. Hope feels like something positive once again, not like a stick to beat myself with. I am forgiving myself. My inner dialogue is kinder.

New Zealand was an amazing trip of a lifetime, but I was eager to get back. I wanted to get the build started to have our two extra bedrooms for our little siblings and start the process to get them. Adoption was starting to feel part of me. Ironic word I know. I think it was part of my journey of acceptance. Adoption was my new pregnant. It would make me a mum. My brain was starting to reframe my story.

I couldn't wait to meet my children. I felt so much love for them.

My life was going to start this year.

Acknowledgements

I would like to thank my Mum and dad, my sister and my Gran for providing a memorable and safe childhood which included some very magical moments and has always been my driver to share this experience of closeness and love with my own children.

For my friends who listened, even when they didn't fully understand.

Thank you to J & J for reading the final draft of this book.

Thank you to my friend Sam who created the beautiful cover to this book.

Thank you to my Counsellor, who gently allowed me to tell my story and showed me how to finally accept my grief.

Thank you to Gary Ward, who thoughtfully edited this book.

For Becky at Defining Mum, who published my very first blog when this book was still in its first draft and my confidence about it was waivering.

Printed in Great Britain
by Amazon

58273806R00172